6

# The *N*ATURE *of* *G*AME

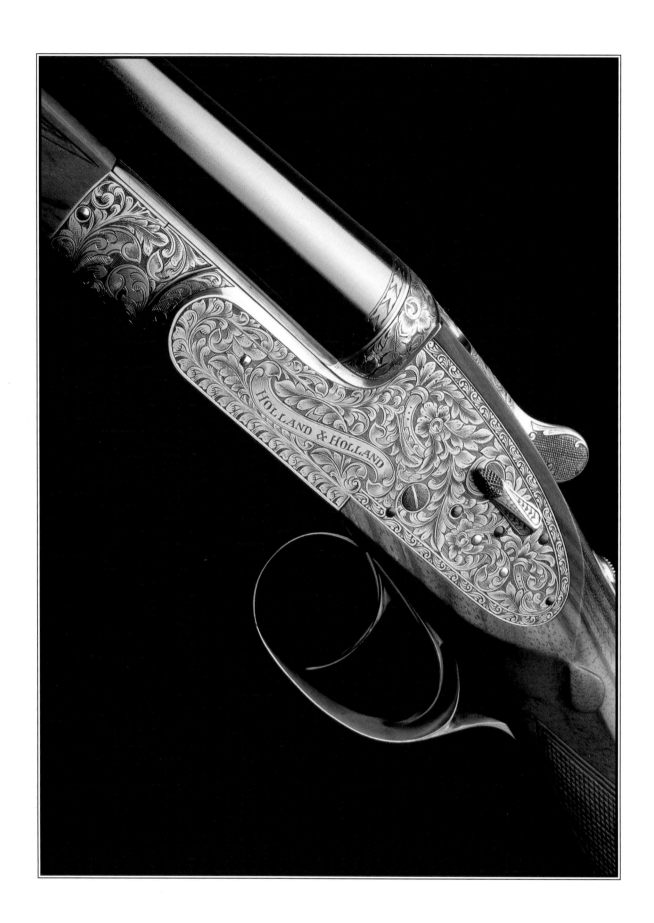

# The NATURE of GAME

*United Kingdom – Europe – North America*
*with*
**HOLLAND & HOLLAND**

## BEN HOSKYNS
*Illustrated by Ben Hoskyns*

*Foreword by*
*HRH The Duke of Edinburgh*

Quiller Press

FOR SALLY
*Small compensation*
*for such a trying start*
*to married life.*

First published 1994 by
Quiller Press Limited
46 Lillie Road
London SW6 1TN
ISBN 1 870948 92 0

799.25 HOS

Designed by Tim McPhee
Produced at Book Production Consultants Plc,
Cambridge, for Quiller Press
Typeset by Cambridge Photosetting Services
Origination by Classic Scan, Singapore
Printed and bound by Kyodo

# CONTENTS

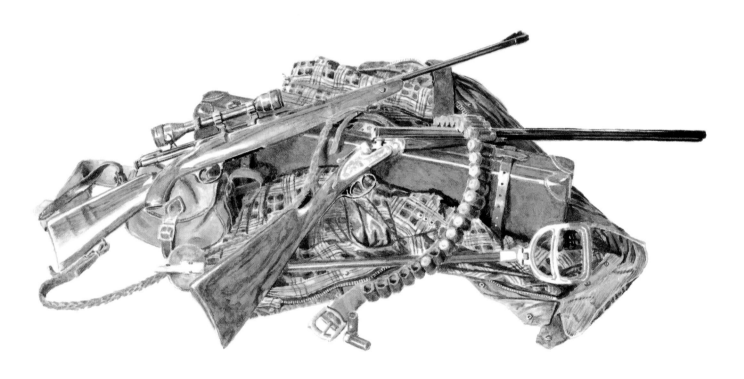

There is much concern in these days about the taking of wild animals for sport, but against that must be placed the protection given to wild habitats and many other wild species in the process of keeping game. It is also true to say that it has often been through shooting, stalking and hunting that many people have come to appreciate the need for the conservation of nature.

Nothing is perfect in this world and it has to be acknowledged that there have been times when the persecution of pest species has been over-done. Those days are over, but many people are beginning to experience the consequences. The explosion in the populations of magpies, crows, raptors and foxes has joined the influence of pesticides, herbicides and fungicides to substantially reduce the numbers of songbirds and ground-nesting waterfowl and waders.

As with everything in nature, it is all a question of balance and this balance can only be achieved by knowledge and understanding. I hope this book will help many people to gain a better understanding of conservation and of the need for the wise and sustainable use of wildlife.

# *Introduction*

MY FIRST WOODCOCK TURNED out to be a green plover. The unfortunate bird flopped, heavy-winged over the hedge and out of the dusk, following the route the woodcock always took. Such was my eagerness to collect my first pin feather, the discreet little pop of the .410 sounded a fraction of a second later. And such was my shame, I left the bird behind. A mistake, perhaps, but that is no excuse. I regret both the shot and the intention of shooting an unsuspecting flighting woodcock.

I have since seen, amongst others, a fieldfare mistaken for a teal; a starling for a snipe; a duck tufted (in the hand) for a shoveler and, once or twice, a bird picked without the gun having a clue to its identity. Quite simply, if the gun cannot correctly identify the quarry, the shot should not be taken. The initial objective of this book is to help with that identification and I hope that my illustrations are accurate enough to be of some use. I decided against silhouettes of flying birds as everyone forms their own picture of flight patterns and identification usually comes from the way a bird moves, as opposed to a frozen image. I have also tried to avoid call descriptions, other than a few of those commonly used, for they are almost impossible to imagine from written expressions. The words 'go back', for example, only make sense once the grouse's call has been heard. Calls are particularly important when duck and goose shooting and the gun

should make every effort to learn them. There is no substitute for simply getting out there, without a gun, to watch and listen.

But there is so much more to shooting than recognition and the 'simple' act of pulling the trigger. The fascination, to me at least, is in the habits of these birds and animals – their beauty runs far deeper than their outward appearance. Wiser minds than I possess have tried to explain the naturalist/hunter paradox. Far more difficult to understand, however, are those guns with little interest in wildlife. The book will hopefully encourage shooting men and women to learn about the birds and animals they pursue and, more importantly, respect them. Naturally there are no hard and fast rules regarding animal behaviour and I have tried not to cast the facts in stone. The one thing that is guaranteed is their ability to prove you wrong.

The book covers all the legal quarry species in Great Britain and Northern Ireland, except those for which a special licence is required. I have also included a selection of birds and animals hunted in continental Europe and North America (excluding Mexico), which should be of general interest to most readers, especially those who wish to travel further afield for their shooting.

Whilst some of the species seem to be faring remarkably well, there is a sad undercurrent, throughout much of the book, with many of the most important gamebirds declining. Generally, it is no longer shooting that is to blame but habitat loss, especially through modern farming practices. Indeed, shooting usually has a positive effect for it is in our own interests to preserve the habitat, and much wildlife, other than game benefits as a result – fortunately. However, the shooting world is quick to point out how much it does for wildlife by way of conservation, when in reality most are simply resting on the laurels of the dedicated minority.

Naturally I have received a considerable amount of help over the habits, management aspects and shooting practices relating to this diverse collection of birds and animals. That such highly respected and busy people should willingly give up their time to talk to me is a reflection of their desire to promote a more respectful and responsible attitude in the shooting field. Any factual errors will be mine. I am especially grateful to the following for their help with the British and European species:

Mark Andrew
Dr David Baines of the Game Conservancy
Hugh Blakeney
Colin Blanchard of the B.A.S.C.
Arthur Cadman
Prue Coats
John Dell
Denny Ellander
Bill Gallant
Will Garfit
Major Iain Grahame of the Daws Hall Trust
Tom Gullick
Barry Hone
Dr Andrew Hoodless of the Game Conservancy
Dr Peter Hudson of the Game Conservancy
John Humphreys
Dr Yves Lecocq of F.A.C.E.
Bill Makins of the Pensthorpe Waterfowl Trust
Dr Robert Moss of the Institute of Terrestrial Ecology
Roddy Petley
Richard Prior
Dr Peter Robertson of the Game Conservancy
William St Aubyn
Dr Adam Watson of the Institute of Terrestrial Ecology

I am greatly indebted to Bob Robel for providing invaluable guidance and introducing me to many of the following from whom I gleaned so much information in respect of the North American species. Most are top biologists and I must apologise for becoming so confused about their titles that I decided to omit them.

Leonard Brennan          James E. Miller
Glen Chambers            Lyman Nichols, Jr.
Kevin E. Church          James M. Peek
Michael Conover          Wayne R. Porath
Alan Crossley            Gary Robbins
Thomas V. Dailey         Donald H. Rusch
Ken Davies               David R. Schad
Elmer J. Finck           Bill Stremmel
Bert Klineberger         Robert K. Swihart
Eric W. Kurzejeski       William Wishart

And finally, my thanks also go to Quiller Press and Holland and Holland, who were trusting enough to let me get on with it, undisturbed.

BEN HOSKYNS, SUFFOLK

# Great Britain and Northern Ireland
## QUARRY SPECIES

PRESENTED WITH A LIST of the legal quarry species of Great Britain and Northern Ireland, it may not always be apparent, especially to the novice, why certain birds and animals are allowed to be shot. It is important, therefore, to include everything – not just those species that are considered 'game' but also the pests and predators, explaining why there is a need for their control.

There may be some who will be surprised to see coots and moorhens grouped amongst the pest species – both are protected with a season and were once popular table birds. However, they are now generally shot to control numbers, although many fall to the beginner's .410, pursued as game. Similarly, to the keen hunting man, it may seem sacrilegious to include the fox amongst the pest animals but then, to the keen hunting man, the very idea of shooting a fox will seem a sacrilege. As a hunted animal, the fox is perceived as game; when it is shot, it is generally considered vermin. Simply labelling birds or animals 'vermin' does not make them any less fascinating and they should be treated with equal respect, controlled legally and humanely.

It is clearly necessary, when dealing with such a varied list of birds and animals, to arrange them in relevant categories. Most of the following species fall within logical groups – gallinaceous birds, waders, geese, ducks etc. The species within the groups also require some structuring and they are, for the most part, arranged in order of importance. However, on a whim, I chose not to launch straight in with a major bird such as the pheasant or red grouse, although I felt that the gallinaceous birds, being the most intensively managed, should be dealt with first. As a native bird and one whose status is generally regarded as a barometer for game birds in this country, the grey partridge should, perhaps, be discussed before the introduced redleg. However, the latter has become far more significant as a quarry species in recent years and the annual bag is considerably larger.

Whilst it is hopefully made clear within the text, it is important to point out that the inclusion of a bird or animal in this section does not necessarily mean that it may be shot in both Great Britain *and* Northern Ireland. There are several species which are fully protected in Northern Ireland whilst allowed in Great Britain and vice versa. As a point of interest, most of the species on the British list are also found and hunted on the continent and, to a lesser extent, in North America – the pheasant, grey partridge, snipe and most of the duck species – although, obviously, they have not been duplicated within those sections.

# GALLINACEOUS BIRDS

## Capercaillie (*TETRAO UROGALLUS*)

DUE PRIMARILY TO LOSS of habitat and over-shooting, the capercaillie became extinct in the British Isles towards the end of the 18th century. Previously found in England and Ireland as well as Scotland, it was successfully re-introduced in Perthshire in 1837 from Swedish stock.

However, the removal of the favoured natural pine forest has continued, mature plantations have been felled and predators have increased. Together with bad weather and numerous deer fence collisions, caper-caillie have been declining since the 1970s.

Due to its enormous size, the capercaillie is unlikely to be confused with any other bird. The mature cock, considerably larger than the hen, is a bluish-black with a brown back and white flecking on the tail and underparts. The hen shows little or no red eyebrow and is similar to the much smaller greyhen but with more obvious barring. The tails of cocks and hens are rounded whilst those of black grouse are forked. However, caper/black grouse hybrids have been known and could cause some confusion.

Capercaillie prefer mature, natural and open coniferous forest with mixed aged trees. However, they will use thicker plantations, especially if made good with clearings promoting heathers and blaeberries. The Scots pine is the most important tree in their habitat and blaeberries the most important part of the undergrowth. Water and grit are also necessary.

Capercaillie may visit arable land near the forest but will not often be found above the tree line and with snow covering the ground, most of the day will be spent feeding in the trees. Nearly 100% of their winter diet consists of pine needles (though sitka spruce can feature significantly) whilst leaves, berries and other seeds are eaten in summer.

Display is complex but, typically, the cock holds his head and neck vertically, with the tail fanned and upright, and a quiet song resembling the sound of a cork being withdrawn from a bottle is made after a series of clicking noises.

Displaying can occur at almost any time of year but activity peaks in late April and early May. The leks, sited in the forest, are traditional and split into displaying territories. Cocks display mostly at dawn before moving to a day time territory adjoining the lek. First year cocks will not take a territory and, generally, hens will come to the highest ranking cock, though they may visit several leks. The territorial birds are extremely aggressive and older cocks will, occasionally, attack humans. Fighting at the lek is common and fatalities often occur.

About 5–12 eggs are laid in a shallow scrape, often at the base of a tree, in late April or May. A replacement clutch will occasionally be laid if the nest is predated but not if the brood is lost. Chicks need a predominantly insect diet for the first 3–4 weeks and can fly at about 2 weeks. Hens are full grown at 3–4 months but the cocks continue to grow for 2 years or more. Generally roosting in trees, capercaillie can sometimes burrow under the snow to

*Cock displaying*

roost at night. Foxes, pine martens and eagles will all  prey on capercaillie to a small extent.

Outside the breeding season, capercaillie cocks are usually solitary though the hens are often found in small groups of 2 or 3. Adults are fairly sedentary but young hens can disperse up to 30km or so. Thus hens tend to colonise new areas with the cocks eventually following.

With widespread management – preserving the natural forest, adjusting the plantations to suit their needs, predator control and even advertising the deer fences by tying strips of plastic to the wire to reduce the risk of fatalities and injuries by collision – it is possible that the capecaillie can survive. The estimated winter population is only about 3500 birds with the main strongholds in Deeside, Speyside and Perthshire.

SEASON: *October 1 – January 31*

There has been a voluntary ban on capercaillie shooting for the past 3 years and the majority of estates are abiding by it. Despite the importance of the revenue for their continued management, it would be pointless if the last few birds were shot before they could benefit from it.

Prior to the ban, the majority of capercaillie were driven. One of the hardest birds to drive, they can fly in any direction when flushed. Guns are often placed behind a tree or root and must keep still and quiet. Drives, which are sometimes for both capercaillie and blackgame, may be a mile long or only a few hundred yards and birds will often flush from the trees – even when they have been feeding on the ground they may fly up into a tree upon hearing the beaters approach. Thick snow can be a problem as the weighted branches hanging down can both hide them and make it difficult for them to flush. Once flushed, capercaillie fly fast and silently with slower wingbeats than blackgame and the deception frequently results in misses.

Another, and often frowned upon method was the stalking of displaying cocks (in season) with a rifle. Supposedly oblivious to everything when its head was stretched upwards, the stalker's approach has been likened to a game of grandmother's footsteps.

Most capercaillie are shot as trophies though young hens can make good eating providing the crop is removed as soon as possible.

*Hen*

*Blackcock*

# Black Grouse (TETRAO TETRIX)

BLACK GROUSE, OR BLACKGAME, once found almost throughout Britain, are now restricted to Scotland, Wales and the North of England. Largely due to loss of habitat, their numbers continue to decline overall, though there may be some local stability.

The beautiful blackcock has a glossy bluish-black plumage with white undertail coverts, wing-bars and patches on the leading edges of its wings. The lyre-shaped tail is fanned outwards in display exposing the white undertail coverts in sharp contrast. The greyhen is similar to the capercaillie hen but smaller, less heavily barred, with a slightly forked tail and a thin white wing-bar.

*Greyhen*

The cock has prominent red eyebrows whilst the hen's are barely noticeable.

A bird of the forest/moorland edge, not often found above the timberline, the ideal habitat for blackgame is open forest – often modest-sized woodland, broken up by bogs and rough openings with an undergrowth of heather. A preference for young, regenerating forest, blackgame will move on as it thickens up and, consequently, man's plantations have helped to slow the decline. Clearings in coniferous forest usually promote the natural regeneration of birch scrub which provides an important winter food, though conifers are also used. The value of such clearings is currently being studied.

When snow covers the ground, arboreal feeding becomes necessary with birch buds and catkins being the preferred winter food. When ground feeding is possible, blackgame feed on shoots, seeds and berries with heather being the most important part of the diet. Arable land is also used, especially when stubbles are available. Blackgame roost both in trees and on the ground, in heather or rushes, and can form snow holes for warmth at night.

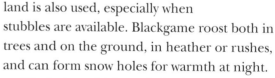

Displaying, which peaks in the spring, can occur at any time of the year though not usually in July and August. The lek is traditional, roughly an acre in size, depending on the number of birds attending, and usually sited in open, grassy areas in woodland clearings and field corners. It is a communal display ground, split into small territories and blackcock do not hold separate territories away from it. Unless ousted, the cock will generally keep the territory for life. Displaying, usually only at the lek, begins before sunrise and continues for an hour or so. Hens visit the lek in the spring and tend to come to the dominant cocks, of which there may be 2 or 3 present and holding central territories. No harem is formed and hens visit purely for mating.

The hen lays 6–12 eggs in mid to late May in a scrape in the ground amongst thick cover and will re-nest if the eggs are predated during the early stages of incubation. The chicks, reared by the hen alone and fairly dependent on insects for the first 2–3 weeks, can fly short distances at 10 days and are independent at about 3 months when the brood splits up. Yearling cocks are unlikely to hold a territory at the lek in their first spring though both cocks and hens are sexually mature by then. Crows are major predators of the nest, as with most gamebirds, and foxes, peregrines and goshawks will all take adult black grouse – goshawks being especially important in Scandinavia and central Europe.

Outside the breeding season, coveys are often mixed, cocks and hens, and in winter, de-pending on the population density, can be very large. In parts of their European range, black-game can 'migrate' 200–300 miles but it is unlikely that any seasonal movement occurs in Britain.

The decline is thought to be due, mainly, to habitat loss through forest maturation.

Blackgame clearly benefit from young plantations and it is possible that clear-felling areas within older forestry may also help. However, other factors may be involved. Overgrazing at the forest edge by sheep and increased red deer numbers may be reducing vegetation to such an extent that black grouse are more prone to predation. This may also be removing an insect-rich habitat upon which the chicks depend. Predation clearly plays a part and blackgame populations appear to be stable where keepering levels are high. The estimated spring population is about 45,000 birds and the main strongholds are in Perthshire, Angus, eastern parts of the borders and Northumberland.

SEASON: *August 20 – December 10*

Whilst the situation is not as worrying as that of the capercaillie, estates are being careful and some only allow blackcock to be shot.

Young birds make good eating (though not as good as red grouse) but the majority, like capercaillie, are probably shot as trophies. The idea of trophy shooting, to some, is anathema but the welfare of blackgame may depend on it.

Occasionally the odd bird will be shot when walking up or driving red grouse near moorland edges but, generally, blackgame are driven from woodland, flushing fairly readily with the general noise from the beaters. Unpredictable and difficult to drive, their flight is quiet and fast though less so, on both counts, than capercaillie. Both can fly high and are easily missed.

Flighting blackgame to grain stooks in the afternoons at harvest time was once a common and exciting form of shooting but is probably only occasionally practised now on stubbles.

*At the lek*

6

# Red Grouse – (*Lagopus lagopus scoticus* & *Lagopus lagopus hibernicus*)

THE RED GROUSE is considered by most to be a sub-species of the willow grouse. Found in Scotland, Ireland (a separate sub-species), Wales and the north and west of England, grouse are in decline due to increased predation, disease and overgrazing. However, had they not been managed in the first place they would never have reached such high densities and this is therefore a decline from unnaturally high levels. The grouse population is still far higher than it was before man's intervention.

Once widespread on most heather moorland, they have now almost disappeared from Exmoor, Dartmoor and large areas of Wales. Numerous attempts to introduce them to heathlands, such as the Brecklands and New Forest, failed and they were introduced into Belgium but are now thought to be extinct.

Red grouse have a rich rufous plumage with brown wing feathers. From a distance, the sexes are similar but there are two moults in the year and hens generally have heavier markings and can be yellower in the breeding season. Yorkshire keepers call this their 'marmalade plumage' and believe these hens to be in better condition. Some variable white flecking may be visible, especially on the underparts, and the legs and feet are feathered in white. The red combs above the

cock's eyes are most noticeable in the breeding season and the hen can enlarge hers to a small extent but they are usually hidden. Both red grouse and ptarmigan possess long toenails which are shed each year.

Prior to deforestation, grouse inhabited the gaps in the natural forest where they were fairly inaccessible and rarely hunted. Managing the open moorland, by predator control and heather burning, increased both the grouse and their potential as driven game. When Queen Victoria bought Balmoral it became fashionable to own an estate in Scotland and grouse have been the cream of driven shooting ever since.

Red grouse are generally found exclusively on heather moorland, though they could exist in some forestry areas where there is enough heather. Their diet consists almost entirely of the shoots, flowers and seeds of ling heather, though cotton grass is important for the breeding condition of the hen in the spring.

Grouse pair up and establish territories in early October, the cock

*Hen brooding*

7

attempting to set up a territory next to his father's (or on it, if his father has died). There is some evidence that the hen is also territorial but it is the cock that establishes the boundaries in the first place and then attracts the hen. Cocks can, very rarely, be bigamous.

As territories hold all the feeding, some believe that most non-territorial birds will subsequently die over winter from starvation and predation. However, in the autumn, territories can break down during the morning enabling non-territorial birds to feed for the rest of the day. When the snows arrive, territories are abandoned altogether and grouse pack together, flying across the moor looking for areas cleared by the wind so they can feed. In snow the most obvious thing on the moor is a red grouse and therefore packing, through safety in numbers, reduces the risk of predation to an individual. When harsh conditions force them off the hill, they will feed in trees and on arable land and will scrape at the snow a little to reach food.

When roosting, grouse will also form shallow holes in hard snow and deep tunnels in soft snow if the air temperature is very low.

Territories are re-established in the spring once the snows have gone, which may not be until March or April. Rocks or raised mounds within the territory act as lookout platforms whilst the hen is incubating and enable the cock to advertise his presence. The cock's display is mostly aerial and if both birds survive, they will often re-pair the following year.

The nest is sited within the territory and nearly always in thick heather. About 6–10 eggs are laid (though heavily diseased birds may produce as few as 2) and incubation usually begins by the end of April. The hen will re-nest if the eggs are predated in the early stages but as incubation progresses the ability to re-lay decreases and she is unlikely to renest if the brood is lost. The territory begins to break down once the hen starts to incubate but the cock, who plays no part in incubation, will continue to defend an area around the nest.

Both parents rear the brood and, if the hen is killed, the cock will rear them alone. Insects are vital for the first 10–20 days but by 3 weeks the chick's diet is predominantly heather. The young are full grown at 12 weeks and the family

*Cock*

usually breaks up in September and October.

Disease, predation and overgrazing are the main factors affecting grouse populations. It is, perhaps, inevitable that, when densities are high, disease will surface. Two major diseases affect red grouse: strongylosis, caused by the trichostrongyle worm, and louping ill, a virus transmitted by the sheep tick. Louping ill can cause 80% mortality in chicks and research is currently being made into sheep vaccination and other methods of controlling the problem. Strongylosis is largely responsible for the red grouse cycle where increased numbers over a period of years results in a high infection one year with a subsequent crash in the population. The older birds with high worm burdens die, allowing for a gradual recovery. Generally the problem is related to summer rainfall with the wetter moors often showing a greater uptake of parasites. A high worm burden can seriously affect the breeding con-dition of the hen and there is a fairly pre-dictable cycle of 4–6 years on English moors whilst in Scotland it tends to be every 6–10 years.

Medicated grit can help to control the situation and direct dosing can provide immediate relief but only a few moors, at present, are taking such measures.

With the increase in plantations, and therefore predators, and the decrease in keepering activities, predation has become a problem. Major grouse predators include the fox, stoat, peregrine and hen harrier (of chicks) with crows being the main enemy at the nest.

Overgrazing by sheep (and increasingly deer) has accounted for the massive loss of heather moorland and a reduction in the density of sheep is the only solution.

Heather burning is one of the most important management practices. The 'muirburn' is done for two main reasons: to maintain the heather and prevent the return of forestry and to provide different types of habitat – short and long vegetation. Heather burning rejuvenates old, straggly heather and the new growth provides more food. Most burning takes place in the first two weeks of April and areas are burned in rotation which varies from moor to moor, ranging from 10 to 25 years. Some areas, such as steep hillsides, where erosion could result, or where there is a risk of bracken spreading, should not be burned. Strips 15–30 metres wide and as long as possible are thought to be the ideal.

SEASON:
*Great Britain: August 12 – December 10*
*Northern Ireland: August 12 – November 30*

Where there is no human intervention, a pair of grouse may occupy 200–600 acres. With moorland management grouse numbers increased dramatically (if not unnaturally) and can, in good years, reach a density of 600 birds per square kilometre. At such densities there is a large surplus which must be reduced if disease is to be avoided. The revenue from sold grouse days is vital for moorland maintenance upon which much wildlife, other than grouse, depends.

Willow grouse cannot be shown in the same numbers and this, coupled with the fact that it is a wild bird, makes driven grouse in Britain so unique. They can be reared for shooting but, aside from being prohibitively expensive, the fascination with grouse is that they are wild and an 'upland pheasant' is to be avoided at all costs.

In Scotland the stag season, closing on 20th October, determines the end of the grouse shooting. Whilst the birds are stronger in September and October, the stags have to be stalked and, therefore, most grouse will be shot in August and early September. In the north of England, where there are fewer predators and chick survival is higher, the moors are more productive and shooting may continue right up until 10th December to keep them at a healthy level.

Most walking up is done in the early part of the season as, by October, the grouse are very much wilder and harder to control. Classically, pointers or setters range ahead of the guns, locating and holding the covey until the guns catch up. There are few more wonderful sights than that of a dog coming up on point, perhaps 80 or more yards ahead. The southerner, used to somewhat flatter, easier going, will instantly ignore any protesting muscles – at least until the shots are fired and the grouse have whirred away. Some walking up is done without pointing dogs, the guns in a broad line, but for many it is not so magical.

Driven grouse is considered by many to be the most exciting form of shooting. To drive them successfully is an art form with the placing of butts, beaters and flankers all being vital elements. Beaters bring in an enormous area of moorland, gathering the grouse and channelling them towards the guns. Grouse fly along the contours of the hill which can help with the placing of the butts –without which the guns need to be well hidden, frequently placed in a gully over which the grouse are driven. The butts themselves – generally wooden blinds or heather-clad stone constructions – are often sited behind a rise to ensure the grouse are committed by the time they see them. This is also designed as a safety aspect for grouse, as a rule, fly low and invite dangerous shooting. Successful grouse shots take their birds well out in front where they may be skidding across the heather tops but it is essential to know the point when this shot becomes unsafe for the beaters and many shoots will have a whistle, after which birds may only be shot behind.

Other dangers appear in the shape of flanking flags who emerge from the heather to turn the birds back into the drive. They are often the key to a successful drive and their position must always be known to the guns (as must any pickers-up). Equally important are one's neighbouring guns. Accidents happen every year in the shooting field but never more so than on a grouse drive with guns swinging through on a fast approaching covey and shooting straight into the next butt. Many butts have sticks on either side to indicate the safe shooting zone.

If the sight of grouse collecting in front of the butts does not set one's heart racing, the sheer acrobatics of a covey coming at full tilt will. It was considered the pinnacle of achievement, in the days of plenty, to take two birds in front, change guns, and shoot two behind. Today, most people would be happy just to be out there on the hill listening to the grouse calling 'go back'. Driven grouse has, sadly, become too expensive for most of us.

# *Ptarmigan* (*LAGOPUS MUTUS*)

CLOSELY RELATED TO the red grouse, the numerous sub-species of ptarmigan, or rock ptarmigan, are widely distributed in northerly lands such as Scandinavia, Siberia, Greenland, Iceland, Canada and Alaska. The very similar white-tailed ptarmigan is also found in North America though with a more limited range.

In Britain, the ptarmigan is restricted to the highlands of Scotland. Rarely found below 2000ft, the ptarmigan lives in a harsh world with little human interference across much of its range. However, in Scotland, overgrazing by sheep is destroying their limited habitat and causing some decline.

Usually found at higher altitudes than most red grouse, ptarmigan are identified by the amount of white in their plumage and, close

to, a more delicate bill. The wing feathers and underparts remain white throughout the year, during which, they undergo three moults. A mottled brown plumage in summer turns to ashy grey-brown in autumn with more extensive white underparts and variable amounts of white flecking on the face and upper-parts. The legs and feet are feathered in white throughout the year. In winter, ptarmigan generally turn pure white except for the tail feathers and the bill which remain dark. However, occasionally the odd grey feather will be retained in the winter plumage. Cocks will also show a black streak, from the bill through the eye, which is usually lacking in the hens, and display red eyebrows, which are prominent in spring and summer but frequently invisible in winter and generally barely noticeable in hens at any time. The call is a frog-like croak.

The ptarmigan's habitat, high in the mountains, consists of short vegetation and rocks and they only desert it in favour of lower and more sheltered corries in very hard weather. The rocks, an important feature of this bleak and barren landscape, are used to hide from predators and to shelter behind at night. Heather, blaeberry and crowberry are their main foods.

Generally, cocks begin taking territories in March, though this is largely dependent on

*Winter plumage*

*Hen in summer*

more, breaking up again in March or April.

Whilst red grouse fly to areas cleared of snow by the wind, ptarmigan often burrow down to feed and will form snow holes in which to roost. In spring, as the snows disappear, ptarmigan (especially the cocks) can be very obvious to predators such as the fox, eagle and peregrine. Little management is possible other than keeping sheep away.

SEASON: *August 12 – December 10*

Ptarmigan shooting is often extremely hard work and, even where the tops are relatively flat, it is still necessary to get above 2000ft in order to find them. The rocky nature of the terrain rarely allows for a comfortable shooting stance.

They are, very occasionally, driven. Flushed birds may fly straight off the mountainside but some will loyally stick to one hill, flying down and looping back up to pitch at the same level some distance ahead. Thus it is sometimes possible to work them towards waiting guns.

The majority, however, are walked up. They will flush wild

spring weather. Cocks display in their white winter plumage, moulting shortly after mating but the hens, requiring camouflage for nesting, moult earlier. Ptarmigan, in Scotland, are usually monogamous and the hen nests within the territory which breaks down in about May.

The clutch of 5–9 eggs is laid in a shallow depression, often in a fairly open site though nest predation is usually quite low. If the nest is predated, the hen may re-lay but she will not be able to after losing the brood. The young can fly at 10 days and are independent at about 3 months when they will often join up with other birds. As winter approaches, ptarmigan gather into coveys of up to 20 or

*Cock in summer*

in bad weather and are usually found on the sheltered side of the hill. In good weather, they will either sit fairly tight or run ahead of the guns who speed up accordingly. However, ptarmigan have little difficulty in keeping ahead and will eventually flush at extreme range.

It is wise to go with someone who knows the land and understands the weather conditions. Remember, too, that birds shot on the side of the hill can fall far below you resulting in a long retrieve. Care should be taken when using inexperienced dogs.

# Pheasant (PHASIANUS COLCHICUS)

ORIGINALLY FROM ASIA, there is some argument as to whether the Romans or Normans introduced the pheasant to Britain. Responsibility aside, it is thought that they only became established in the wild about 600 years ago. It has adapted to the British climate and habitat remarkably well.

Various different subspecies have been introduced over the years and a great many will and do interbreed and it is unlikely now that there are any pure forms in the wild in Britain, other than ornamental pheasants. This constant crossbreeding has produced endless plumage variations.

The most commonly seen are the so called 'ring neck' and the 'old English' – those with and those without white collars. In simple terms the cocks are a striking orange-gold with glossy green heads and long, olive-brown tails. The red wattles around the eyes are less pronounced outside the breeding season but, generally, clearly visible. There are innumerable variations and combinations in the width of the white collar, the barring on the tail feathers and the colour of the forewing, upper tail coverts, legs, underparts and the crown of the head. The hens, at a cursory glance, appear to be buffish in colour with dark brown markings but these, on closer inspection, can be immensely varied in pattern.

Hens can, occasionally, assume a similar plumage to the cock, usually as a result of damage to the ovaries, resulting in a hormone imbalance. These gynandro-morphs will often show a green head, though not glossy, and a gold body with a few hen feathers mixed in. There are no bright red

*Territorial cock*

wattles, just the touch of pink that a hen normally shows. The body and head are unquestionably hen-shaped.

The melanistic, a mutation, is generally less varied despite the fact that it can come from parents of, apparently, normal colouring – it is not uncommon to see a normal hen leading a mixed brood of chicks. Effectively the cock has a green head and, usually, no white collar though this is not unknown. The body is purple, reflecting blue, with brown wings, tail and tail coverts. The melanistic hen is a dark chocolate brown with pale edged feathers.

Another mutation, often called the bohemian or leucistic pheasant, is becoming increasingly common. The cock's greyish-buff head is not glossy and, whilst it sports the gold body of the normal cock, the breast and flank feathers are tipped with greyish-buff and not black. The bohemian cock may take the ring neck or old English form and, often, a slight purple in the body colour will indicate any melanistic blood. The hen can also show melanistic ancestry, appearing blotched with brown but is otherwise a very pale and finely marked bird and extremely pretty.

There are many other variations – most notably the Japanese green pheasant, a seperate species – but there seems to be no limit to the subtle differences and to continue would be monotonous.

Cock pheasants will start laying claim to territories in late February although half-hearted sparring will occur throughout the winter. Fights rarely become serious and often one bird will back down before a blow has been struck. As the spring progresses the tell-tale double crow and drum of wings from the territorial cock is increasingly heard. Territories vary in size considerably and can cover several acres – usually a mixture of arable and woodland edge. The

more woodland edge, the more possible territories and, consequently, several small, irregularly shaped woods will provide a better potential for breeding success than one large block of forestry.

As the growing crops begin to provide cover in the fields, there is a wide-spread dispersal of birds from their winter haunts and, once the territories have been established, the remaining cocks will, generally, skulk further out in the fields. The two are easily told apart as the territorial struts about his patch with enlarged wattles, erect ear tufts and puffed out feathers. The rather sorry looking non-territorial does not give the crow and drum.

The pheasant is a polygamous bird and, interestingly, once the cock has secured his territory he does not go in search of hens. The hens come to the cocks, deciding which they like the look of most, and it is quite common to see one cock with several hens whilst his neighbour has none. Six hens is about the maximum a cock can guard successfully – though more is by no means uncommon. The cock retains his territory until May or June but plays no part in brood-rearing.

The first eggs will be found in early April, though most clutches are laid in May. Nests are usually sited in moderately thick ground cover in woodland, scrub, hedges or arable crops

*Displaying*

and the hen incubates the 10–18 olive coloured eggs alone. The chicks, able to leave the nest once they are dry, feed almost exclusively on insects for the first 2 weeks. On intensively farmed land such food can be scarce and conservation headlands seem to offer the only ray of hope to wild broods of both pheasants and partridges. These strips around the edges of fields are selectively sprayed, leaving the broadleaved weeds, which benefit the insects the chicks prefer, and can double their survival rate.

At 10 days, the chicks can fly very short distances – often enough to reach thick cover and safety. Although relatively independent at 4 weeks, the brood generally stays together for

about 3 months. Full plumage is attained at 17–18 weeks and they reach adult body weight at about 22 weeks.

A large percentage of hens will renest if the first clutch has been predated and a few will try again if the whole brood is lost but there is no time for a second brood if the hen is successful in rearing the first. Day old chicks seen in October are almost always from a small second clutch when the hen has lost her first nest or brood and, in any event, rarely survive the disappearing insect life and often severe frosts, especially once the hen can no longer brood them.

As the waste grain is ploughed in with the stubbles, pheasants tend to move back to the woods and thick overgrown hedges where they can feed on the mass of autumn berries and acorns. By now most of the wild broods will be following their mothers up to roost in trees

and bushes. Most pheasants choose to spend the night off the ground but it is not uncommon to find them 'jugging' in even quite modest cover and in Fenland, where trees are scarce, it is the norm. During the winter, pheasants take advantage of what food man provides at the hopper, feed ride and in game cover strips. The hens tend to band together in small groups but the more solitary cocks are rarely far away.

Paradoxically, it is man's tender loving care over his pheasants that has weakened the bird's ability to survive. Whether the survival instinct has been bred out of them through countless generations of hand rearing, or purely the fact that the hen chick, hatched in an incubator or, to a lesser extent, by a rather naive and unwary bantam, does not learn that crucial information at first hand, is unclear. The hand reared cock, taking a territory in the spring, seems to have the natural instinct to remain alert and protect his patch, and this constant vigilance offers him, and therefore his hens, considerable forewarning and, thus, protection from predators. The hand reared hen, on the nest or with her brood, shows little indication that she is a fit mother. The odds are against a hand reared pheasant surviving a year, even without shooting, but one must assume that, given the luck of a few near misses by predators, the bird will become a little streetwise and a hen could learn to communicate her fears to her brood. Reared hens do manage to raise broods but there is a considerable amount of luck involved and they are diluting the wild hen population. The releasing and shooting of cocks-only protects the wild hens without the need to reduce shooting pressure and it could significantly increase wild bird production and provide better birds, especially where other game management practices are carried out.

SEASON:

*Great Britain: October 1 – February 1*
*Northern Ireland: October 1 – January 31*
*(cocks only – hen pheasants may be shot under licence obtainable from the Dept. of the Environment, Countryside and Wildlife Branch)*

Driven shooting accounts for the majority of the annual bag of pheasants in Britain. This can vary, from very informal half beat/half stand days when you may get a few shots, to extremely efficient and calculated shoots with keepers, beaters, pickers-up, game-carts and walkie-talkies.

The former, usually managed on a DIY basis, will generally be on a small acreage and, consequently, will have a limited number of drives which can often mean that all the available cover is beaten out each time it is shot. Naturally, such land should only be shot two or three times in a season. At the other end of the scale, the large shoot will begin the season with drives from game cover strips and outlying woods, gradually progressing to their pen woods which need to be stirred up from time to time to encourage the birds into other drives. Some keepers manage to feed their birds out to the surrounding drives so effectively that they never need to shoot their release coverts.

*Bohemian*

In simple terms a straight line of beaters moves slowly through cover flushing the birds steadily from about the middle onwards. Flushed too early, the pheasant, which is not capable of flying great distances, is likely to drop back in before reaching the guns. Without a long rest, it will be extremely reluctant to fly again and, if pushed, will usually dribble out at head height. In a wood with sparse cover and plenty of birds, if they are allowed to run on to the end before getting up, they will come out in large flushes, producing little excitement for all but 2 or 3 guns. Driving pheasants successfully, therefore, is linked inextricably with good woodland management and the placing of the standing guns.

However, it is important to point out that a successful drive does not necessarily mean a mass of very tall pheasants. Placing guns at short-sighted pegs in woodland may not produce tower birds but such snap shooting will often test guns who have become used to more open plan days. Quality shooting is, consequently, not about height but difficulty.

When walking up pheasants, it is essential to have a dog, not for finding and flushing the birds, although it will undoubtedly help, but for retrieving. A wounded

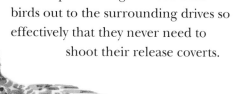

*9 week cock poult - the short tail generally indicates a reared bird*

pheasant can run extremely fast and hide in the thickest of cover. Walking up pheasants – which can be hard work and the few shots well earned – is often done with only one or two guns and their dogs, working smaller areas of more manageable cover than the driven shoot's coverts. Good thick hedges, sugar beet, scrubland and boggy reedbeds will often produce the odd bird but the excitement is in the unpredictability, when compared with driven shooting, and the pleasure in watching your dog work. The after Christmas pheasant, especially the cock, is somewhat wiser and tends to run at the slightest sound but, though the bag may be small, one remembers every shot, whilst on a large driven day things can become a bit of a blur.

As with any bird, always watch a pheasant you think you may have hit until it is out of sight – it is your job to ensure that the birds you have shot have been marked. There is

nothing more infuriating than to have to stop shooting in order to watch a bird your neighbour hit because he cannot be bothered – pheasants can often fly 200–300 yards before collapsing.

On both walked up and driven days it is important to stop shooting early to allow plenty of time for the birds to feed and go up to roost in peace.

*Hen*

A great many pheasants are released each year in order to guarantee the shooting. Managed carefully they can provide superb, testing targets but they are often over-fed and over-tame and sadly there are still too many people more interested in numbers than quality, though they profess adamantly that it is the other way round.

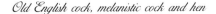

*Old English cock, melanistic cock and hen*

# Red-legged Partridge (ALECTORIS RUFA)

THE RED-LEGGED PARTRIDGE, or Frenchman, was only introduced successfully into Great Britain towards the end of the 18th century, after several failed attempts since the 1670s. Apart from a few scattered populations in Scotland, northern England and Wales, they are generally to be found south of the North Yorkshire Moors – although they have not taken to Devon and Cornwall – and their position strengthens towards the east. The redleg favours well drained mixed farmland and waste ground and has proved more adaptable to modern farming methods than the grey partridge.

The redleg has a dumpy, compact shape with a rather short tail. The head is usually held well down on its shoulders unless running which it does with a more upright gait. The sexes are alike and, from a distance, appear to be an olive-brown. Close up, this covers the cap on its head, back of the neck and upperparts of the body to the tip of the tail where the outer tail feathers are a dull rusty brown. A black stripe cuts through the red-rimmed eye, continuing down and across the front of the neck and breaking up into streaked spots over the chest. Together with the white cheeks and throat and red bill, the redleg has an unmistakable facial pattern. The breast is a greyish-blue as are the flanks which are boldly barred with white, black and dark reddish-brown. The underparts are a pale yellow-orange and the red legs give the bird its name. Knobbly spurs generally indicate a cock but sexing is usually done by weight and neither method is guaranteed.

Flight is generally low with whirring wingbeats, broken by periods of gliding and, whilst they seldom fly further than a few hundred yards, they recover quickly and can repeat a similar length flight almost immediately. The rapid wingbeats give the appearance of a very fast bird but the redleg partridge is in fact slower than the pheasant (the grey being slower still). The call is an unmistakable 'chuck, chuck, chuck-or', with a few similar variations, and 'k-chee, chee' repeated, sometimes monotonously.

There are plumage variations due to the cross breeding of wild redlegs and released chukar hybrids. The true chukar (Alectoris chukar) is very similar in markings and colour but lacks the large amount of black speckling on the chest. However, with yet further cross breeding in the wild, some of these hybrids can look almost identical. The true redleg's flank feathers have only one black bar on each; the chukar cross had two and subsequent hybrids sometimes show single black bars on almost all but one or two feathers. Without the bird in the hand it is usually impossible to tell such similar birds apart. It is now illegal to release the chukar hybrid into the wild.

The covey fragments towards the end of winter when territories are obtained and pair bonds formed. The nest is a scrape in the ground, lined thinly with dead grass, usually in the thick undergrowth of a hedge or

overgrown field corner. The clutch of 10–18 eggs – a variable shade of buff, speckled with reddish-brown – are laid in late April or May with later nests generally being the result of first nest predation. There are occasional instances of double-brooding – the hen laying a second clutch immediately and both parents incubating simultaneously.

The chicks leave the nest shortly after hatching and are reared by both parents but feed themselves. Insects are crucial during the first 2 weeks and a cold, wet early summer is therefore usually disastrous to chick survival. By 10 days they can fly short distances and their chances of survival, in the face of bad weather, insect shortages and predation, increase steadily as they grow with the diet gradually becoming more vegetarian – grain, flowers, buds, weed seeds etc. Adult plumage is attained by about 9–10 weeks.

Redlegs generally sleep on the ground – although sometimes they may roost on the top of barns and farm buildings (especially reared birds). Whilst the grey partridge covey remains a family unit until the spring, the redlegs are often joined by other coveys, broodless pairs or single birds.

Often seen on straw stacks and the large round bales at harvest time, the autumn is really the partridge's time of year. The wild redleg likes to be able to see the land all around and stubble allows it to see, often without being seen. Once the fields have been drilled and rolled they can find little cover or protection from prying eyes, though they still prefer to stay well out in the open, running and then flying at the first sign of danger.

SEASON:

*1st September – 1st February (Northern Ireland: may only be shot under licence obtainable from the Dept. of Environment – Countryside and Wildlife Branch)*

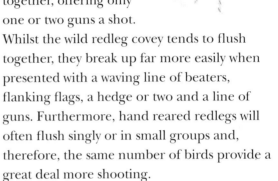

With the advent of the breech loading shotgun, driven game became both possible and practical. However, the grey partridge's characteristics did not lend themselves well to driven shooting – the covey generally flushing and flying together, offering only one or two guns a shot. Whilst the wild redleg covey tends to flush together, they break up far more easily when presented with a waving line of beaters, flanking flags, a hedge or two and a line of guns. Furthermore, hand reared redlegs will often flush singly or in small groups and, therefore, the same number of birds provide a great deal more shooting.

Wild redlegs are not easily walked up, especially once the stubbles have been ploughed, and a lot of time can be wasted chasing coveys across the countryside in the hope that, eventually, they will drop into cover and allow a stealthy approach. If you are lucky you will catch them in a strip of cover, such as maize or sugar beet, when they are feeding but generally they come out again into the open, once fed, enabling them to watch your approach from afar.

Walking up wild redlegs, even in the stubbles, is not particularly successful but you may get the odd long shot especially as a flanking gun walking ahead of the line. In cold weather they can often be surprised in sheltered field corners, thick hedges or scratching around in the bottom of ditches while the open fields are frozen hard. They can even burst out of a little spinney (often making use of pheasant feeders) but they will flush very wild.

*Chukar cross flank*

*Redleg flank feather*

Hand reared redlegs, like pheasants, can become extremely tame. Not having the natural, inbred, survival instinct of their wild counterparts they can usually be approached in cover strips without much difficulty and often flush individually, regrouping later as a covey. Normally when caught out in the open, they can be run into cover, only flushing when the threat of danger is close, making both walked up and driven shooting a lot more predictable, though driving partridges remains an art form.

To drive partridges successfully you need to know where your coveys are at any given time of day, where they will be found in adverse weather conditions and their preferred route of escape when flushed. Some partridge drives can be likened to gathering up grouse from a large area of moorland, bringing the birds in and channelling them towards the guns. Several fields are brought in by, to begin with, very well spaced beaters all gradually aiming for the hedge in front of the guns. The wind plays a significant role – without it the birds trickle through the line, often too low for safety. Even a little wind can make a remarkable difference and a strong one will show very challenging birds but the organiser must be flexible and prepared to move the line of guns and/or the beaters,

*Immature*

even to the extent of taking the drive in the opposite direction.

Get to your peg, keep quiet and be patient – if it is a long drive it may be quite a while before you see the first birds as early flushes will often pitch back in nearer the guns. There will usually be a whistle which will signify that the beaters are in position. Do not shoot before the whistle as it could seriously upset the outcome of the drive. At the same time, birds may show very shortly after the whistle and many people are caught out, having stopped to natter with their neighbour. There is another golden rule of partridge shooting and this also applies to the partridge drive thrown in as an extra on a pheasant day: where partridges are expected, shoot only at partridges unless you have been specifically told that you may shoot anything else. Often as not, the line of guns are well hidden behind a thick hedge and cannot see coveys building up on the other side. Usually it is the gun on the end of the line, expecting little to come his way, who takes an ambitious shot at a high pigeon and watches, with an empty gun, as a covey breaks out from the corner of the hedge and whirrs away across the field.

Mark your shot birds well – landing on their fronts they can be very difficult to see, even in relatively short grass and lightly touched partridges will often be found dead in the next field.

# Grey Partridge (PERDIX PERDIX)

THE NATIVE GREY, or English, partridge is, in Britain, at the edge of its natural range though it has been introduced into North America, where it is often called the Hungarian partridge. Being dependent on good summers for breeding success, it is extremely vulnerable to the unpredictable British climate. Found almost throughout the British Isles, including lower moorland edges, the grey partridge does best on light, well drained, mixed arable land.

From a distance grey and redleg partridges are hard to tell apart, being very similar in shape, but, on closer inspection, there can be no confusion. The cock has a pale tawny face, mottled brown cap and grey neck, chest and flanks which are barred with reddish-brown. The brown upper parts are barred and streaked with chestnut and buff and the belly is white with a dark chestnut breast patch, roughly resembling an upside down horseshoe. The hen is very similar though the face seems more washed out and, usually, a few faint chestnut smudges replace the horseshoe. The actual markings on the wing coverts and scapular feathers are also different but the birds need to be compared in the hand to notice this. The call is a creaking 'Kirr-it' with the last syllable often repeated, especially when flushed.

The habits of the grey partridge are very similar to the redleg. The coveys tend to break up a little earlier, in late January and early February as the birds pair and establish territories. The once common practice of walking up partridges allowed a more selective method of shooting. By culling the older and more aggressive birds, a higher spring density could, theoretically, be maintained.

The nest, a scrape in the ground, is sited in the moderately thick grassy or weedy vegetation of banks and hedge-bottoms or amongst growing crops and grassland. The hen lays a clutch of about 15–18 olive coloured eggs – similar to the pheasant's but much smaller – in late April-early May and will often renest in the event of predation by foxes and corvids etc. Some 6–7 weeks will elapse between laying the first egg and hatching and nests are extremely vulnerable to predation.

The chicks, tended by their courageous and attentive parents, leave the nest shortly after hatching and, in common with other gamebirds, are dependent on an insect diet for the first 2–3 weeks. When the poults no longer need brooding at night the birds will roost together on the ground, facing outwards from a circle. The poults attain adult plumage

Hen

at about 8 weeks and the covey stays together as a family unit through to the following January when the cycle is repeated.

The grey partridge has suffered a serious decline since the war and this cannot be solely attributed to poor weather during Royal Ascot week, which is roughly when the main hatch occurs. Whilst weather does play a part in breeding success, the most important factors contributing to the grey's downfall are predators and modern farming practices.

As gamekeepers have themselves suffered a decline, so has predator control. Many shoots rely too heavily on reared birds, to the extent that wild game is often neglected in the spring and predators dealt with mainly at the time of release. The shoots with good numbers of wild partridges realise the importance of looking after them. It is those with only the odd pair that find little inclination to protect them. Here the little grey partridge struggles to survive, barely producing enough young to cover the expected winter losses and provide a breeding stock for the following spring, even without shooting.

The removal of thousands of hedgerows saw the massive loss of nesting habitat. With the hedges went little copses and rough scrubland as every 'spare' inch of land went under the plough. This efficient farming further compounded the problem by the intense use of herbicides which removed the broadleaved weeds, beneficial to the insects which are so crucial to the survival of partridge chicks. As if this was not enough, the cutting of silage, hay and set-aside accounts for a large number of nests and often the hen is also killed.

Recovery is possible in the areas where the grey was once common, given the combination of dry summers, effective predator control, provision of nesting cover and conservation headlands. Quite aside from the shooting, the mere thrill of hearing these beautiful birds calling at dusk is worth every effort and their presence is a sign of successful game management.

SEASON:
*Great Britain: September 1 – February 1*
*Northern Ireland: fully protected*

The grey partridge will sit tight as a covey, even in quite sparse cover, and stubbles, left unploughed, allow the traditional form of shooting partridges over dogs as well as providing excellent holding cover on the driven shoot. Generally, when walking-up, the first birds to rise from a covey are the adults and this theoretically enables them to be shot selectively. In practice, the excitement causes things to become rather blurred but if just the single birds and barren pairs are taken, a higher proportion of young will be left for the following breeding season.

As the redleg found its niche as a driven bird, attention switched away from the grey which always flushes as a covey and cannot provide the same amount of shooting. Consequently, relatively few people rear the grey and whilst the hand reared bird, like the redleg and pheasant, does not make much contribution to wild breeding, for some it may be the only way to see them. The reared greys rarely tame like the redleg. They are extremely skittish and retain the characteristic of flushing as a covey and a few released will add a spark of excitement and variety, offering the guns a wonderful sight if not a shot or two.

*Flank*

*Cock*

*Tail*

*Scapular*

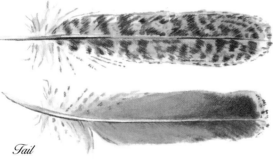

Whilst the same methods of driving are used, this little bird, which is so similar in many ways to the redleg, provides a very different and infinitely more exciting form of shooting. Redlegs, though they fly faster, do not have the same explosive agility that the greys possess when they top the hedge and see the guns. That sight has to be worth preserving.

# WADERS

## *W*oodcock *(SCOLOPAX RUSTICOLA)*

ALTHOUGH THE WOODCOCK generates enormous interest in the shooting field it, nevertheless, remains shrouded in mystery. The subject of much conjecture in the past, research is only just beginning to get to grips with this elusive bird.

The majority of woodcock found throughout the British Isles are winter visitors. There is, however, a resident breeding population which is almost as equally widespread except in western areas of Britain and Ireland, where the winter densities are high. The overall winter population is thought to be increasing and the resident population stable.

Rarely seen on the ground, it is usually a silhouetted flight pattern rather than plumage which identifies them. To see a live woodcock close up for more than a few brief seconds is a memorable experience. Whilst marvelling at the complexities of its plumage, one's attention is constantly drawn to the huge liquid black eye. Set high on the sides of its head, the woodcock's eyes enable it to see fully 360 degrees with only two small blind spots to the front and rear.

The woodcock's plump, dumpy and short-necked appearance avoids any confusion with other long-billed waders and even in the air it has a compact, solid look with somewhat rounded wings which give the bird a deceptively slow and ponderous flight. The

*Breast*

*Tail covert*

*Tail*

initial flush produces a rattle of wings, after which, flight is silent.

The sexes are alike and apart from the eyes and long bill, the most noticeable markings are the broad dark bars on the crown and back of the head. The rest of the back and upper wing coverts comprise the rich pattern of dark browns, russets and creams which blend so perfectly with the leaf litter on a woodland floor. The underparts are pale with a fine dark barring and the undersides of the dark tail feathers are tipped with pure white.

There are some rare colour variations but the most talked about oddity is the short-billed woodcock. Once thought to be the result of injury, its increasing occurrence cannot be explained. For a bird so dependent on probing soft ground to reach food, the evolving of a shorter bill is strange to say the least. The woodcock's main food is the

earthworm which, in dry weather, can be some distance underground. However, the recorded specimens have apparently proved to be in good condition and, thus, unaffected by the abnormality.

Most of our wintering woodcock return to Scandinavia and the Baltic states in March. In Britain, late winter will show early preparations for the coming breeding season with males chasing each other and calling – 'twisick' – at dusk but the 'roding' display flight of the male

25

usually begins in March and continues through the spring and much of the summer. Once thought to be monogamous, research has found that dominant males will breed with several females in succession, taking another mate once incubation begins, and the roding flight is used to advertise his presence to females on the ground. Displaying in the early evenings and to a lesser extent at dawn, the flight of the roding male is generally unhurried and direct, just above the tree tops, and the bird makes frog-like croaks and 'twisicking' calls. The dominant males make these display flights but it is believed that no territory is defended.

The preferred nesting site is in deciduous woodland with moderate ground cover though the nest itself is often ill-concealed and the pale eggs clearly visible. Usually 4 eggs are laid in a scantily leaf and grass-lined depression between April and June though nests have been found considerably earlier and later. Believed to only have one brood in the year, late clutches may well be the result of first nest predation.

Incubation and brood rearing is by the female alone and the young, fed initially with regurgitated food, are capable of leaving the

nest within a few hours. There is considerable argument as to whether the female, for whatever reason – to overcome obstacles, avoid predators or reach better feeding – can carry her young. As with ghosts, many people dismiss the idea until they have seen it but it is difficult to doubt the hundreds of eye-witness accounts.

Most of the corvids are a serious threat at the nest especially early in the breeding season when ground cover is sparse. Sparrowhawks, foxes and stoats are amongst the main predators of both adults and young though the woodcock's camouflage, habits and all-round vision must offer it considerable protection.

Large numbers of woodcock come to Britain each autumn to avoid the harsh winter weather conditions of their breeding grounds. The full moon at the end of October or early November, often called the 'woodcock moon', is traditionally the time of their arrival and most pause briefly to recover amongst the east coast coverts before dispersing across the rest of the British Isles. As winter progresses, hard frosts will drive large numbers of woodcock to the milder areas of western Britain and Ireland. However, moderate frosts are less of a problem to woodcock than to snipe and many shoots in other parts of Britain see increased numbers where they have damp, well sheltered pasture, ditches and woods only to lose them again in milder weather.

Woodcock are secretive birds, flighting out to feed at dusk and returning, often to the same roost, at dawn. They, therefore, favour quiet woodland with access to permanent pasture nearby. The relatively frost-free west, with its high rainfall and large acreages of grazed, worm-rich pasture, combined with good roosting cover, offers the ideal winter habitat. On the best woodcock shoots pheasants are not encouraged for they are noisy birds, active when woodcock are resting, and their coverts are disturbed too frequently by shooting and keepering activity.

Whilst woodcock rarely roost in very thick cover, they appreciate the warmth and security  of dense vegetation around them. Managing woodcock coverts is about providing access both for the birds and the guns or beaters. Woodcock generally roost fairly close to an edge of some sort and provision of rides increases that edge as well as allowing easy entrance and exit at dawn and dusk and escape routes when disturbed.

SEASON:
*September 1 – January 31 (Scotland)*
*October 1 – January 31 (elsewhere)*

Across much of Britain, woodcock shooting has traditionally been opportunistic – guns taking advantage of a sudden 'fall' of 'cock – but where they can be found in high numbers, especially when hard weather prevails else-where, driven shooting becomes possible.

Woodcock are unpredictable and difficult to drive successfully. Aside from the possibility that they may have moved on before the shooting day has arrived, they cannot be controlled like pheasants. There is, perhaps, a preference to flush ahead and away from the beaters but whether they will fly to the standing guns is another matter. Rarely flying great distances when flushed, woodcock will often drop back into the same wood a couple of hundred yards ahead. Drives are, therefore, frequently short and the longer coverts may be broken up into consecutive drives. With several walking guns and a few standing, such short drives offer less routes of escape. On the assumption that a woodcock always reserves the right to change its mind and escape at the sides of the covert, the walking guns are often encouraged to take birds flying forwards. Generally placed along rides or close to the woodland edge to avoid the risk of turning the birds, the standing guns need to be ready for quick snap-shots at all times.

On some drives the whole line of guns may be moving along rides and it is essential to be aware of these constantly changing positions. Woodcock are agile birds and have remarkable acceleration especially when missed with the first barrel. They can dive low to the ground or, sometimes, straight at your head and change direction with the briefest flick of the wing and, such is the joy of connecting, this can make them one of the most dangerous birds to shoot, whether driven or walked up.

Most woodcock in western Britain are walked up. They are rarely found in sufficient numbers eleswhere to warrant specific woodcock days but in the west they are often the staple quarry of the rough-shooter. Woodcock are often seen to flush quite readily with the general noise of people moving through cover but they can, at times, sit very tight and dogs are invaluable for working the thick brambles and essential for retrieving this superbly camouflaged bird. However, it has been known, especially with wounded birds, for woodcock to completely lose their scent and totally bewildered dogs have been seen literally standing over a bird on bare ground watching their handler's frantic commands to complete the retrieve. Some dogs refuse to pick woodcock and snipe, apparently finding the taste unpleasant.

A large proportion of the annual woodcock bag in Britain are shot as incidentals on driven pheasant days. Some shoots may only provide the odd bird whilst others regularly produce half a dozen or more but they will always generate interest, excitement and anticipation, and superb pheasants are usually over-shadowed, even by an 'easy' woodcock.

*Wing primary*

*Pin feather*

*Scapular*

## Snipe *(GALLINAGO GALLINAGO)*

WHILST SNIPE ARE FOUND widespread throughout the British Isles, both as residents and winter visitors, very few remain to breed in the south-west of either England or Wales. The main breeding grounds are in Iceland, Scandinavia and the Baltic States but, of our 720,000 wintering birds, some 40,000–50,000 pairs remain to nest in Britain. The snipe's dramatic decline since the 1950s is generally attributed to the extensive field and marsh drainage carried out to increase agricultural productivity. The decline has slowed in recent years but is thought to be continuing.

Snipe are very small birds and, as such, are often overlooked. However, when flushed they rise powerfully, demanding attention with their rasping call: 'scaap'. They are beautifully camouflaged with mottled brown upperparts, striped with buff; a white belly and barred

There are some who position themselves on traditional routes and shoot flighting woodcock at dusk. If the woodcock are 'in' these flight-lines are almost guaranteed and the birds are unlikely to see the gun in the gloom below, but there are many who consider that woodcock deserve better and liken this to the custom in some parts of Europe of shooting roding woodcock in spring. It is said that this latter form of shooting is not easy and that nearly all the birds shot are males and, consequently, being a polygamous bird, breeding is not affected. But it is also generally agreed that roding woodcock fly much more slowly and directly, leading one to wonder how difficult the shooting really is. More importantly, however, roding woodcock are the dominant males and those that are shot are replaced from a pool of non-roding, sub-dominant and, therefore, inferior birds. The genetic effects of this may never emerge and woodcock, at present, appear to be healthy and increasing in Great Britain but the implications are plain to see in a world where 'survival of the fittest' and selection in the breeding process are thought to be so important.

*Axillary*

flanks. Two broad dark stripes run along the crown and another through the eye which, like that of the woodcock, is set well back on the head to allow for rearward vision whilst feeding. Compared with the woodcock, the bill is longer and both body size and its more delicate shape allow for easy identification between the two. The snipe is most easily confused with the smaller jack snipe (protected in Great Britain, though still legal quarry in Ireland) and the larger great snipe – a rare and fully protected visitor. The jack snipe has a shorter bill, different crown pattern, dark tail and broader yellowish-buff stripes along its back. In flight, it is less erratic, often pitching again a short distance ahead.

The great snipe flies quite directly, is more heavily built and has a barred belly and noticeably white outer tail feathers.

As the winter visitors leave for their breeding grounds between late February and the end of March, the resident males begin to establish territories in reedbeds and moorland bogs and, from late March to June (occasionally as late as July) display with their drumming flights to attract a mate. Diving steeply from a great height with the tail

fanned, a humming sound is produced by the vibration of the two outer tail feathers. Snipe are generally monogamous although both sexes can show a high degree of promiscuity.

The nest is sited in damp areas, usually amongst tussocky grass or tufts of juncus rush, and the clutch of, typically, 4 eggs is laid between April and August, though late nests are relatively uncommon and probably the result of first nest predation. Re-nesting may also be attempted in the event of brood loss, providing it is not too late in the season.

Incubation is carried out by the female, usually once the clutch is complete but occasionally commencing with the penultimate egg. The brood usually splits shortly after hatching, with each parent taking care of two chicks, reared away from each other, presumably to avoid the risk of total loss to predators. The chicks grow quickly, fed initially by the parents with regurgitated food, and start to fly at 19–20 days, becoming independent a few days later. Nest predation is mostly by corvids and, to a lesser extent, foxes and rats whilst adult snipe are taken by both sparrowhawks and merlins.

Little is known about the snipe's feeding behaviour. Their diet consists of earthworms, fly larvae, adult and larval beetles and some seeds and it is generally assumed that once the young can fly, they become rather more nocturnal, flighting to their feeding grounds at dusk and returning at dawn but they certainly feed during the day as well and, during hard weather, it is essential. In winter,

snipe generally roost in bogs and marshes where they may also feed, though they are often found on wet pasture, stubbles and winter cereals at night. In a few undisturbed areas, large numbers may be encountered on such fields during the day where, with little cover, they tend to flush readily making driving more practical. However, this is rather the exception and there are very few estates that can provide more than the occasional snipe drive.

The winter visitors arrive with the full moons between September and December, the majority reaching the favoured west in November, or sometimes as early as October. These tiny birds are highly susceptible to hard weather, unable to tolerate frozen ground for more than 2 or 3 days. Whilst a few may spend the winter on coastal marshes, there are thought to be extensive movements to the predominantly frost-free west and Ireland during periods of prolonged freezing.

The most important management practice is to stop further drainage. The slight shift away from intensive farming may allow some odd corners to revert back to a more favourable habitat. Currently, few bother to actively manage the bogs and marshes for snipe. By cutting small areas of about an acre to create a varied mosaic of open and rushy patches, both breeding and wintering birds would benefit. Cattle should be excluded in the spring, to avoid the risk of nest loss by

trampling, but returned in the early autumn to poach the ground and make it more attractive in winter.

SEASON:
*Great Britain: August 12 – January 31*
*Northern Ireland: September 1 – January 31*

The snipe is, perhaps, the only bird with the wonderful ability to make the very best shots feel a little inadequate. To most there is more than a considerable amount of luck involved in bringing one of the little birds down and eventual success often results in a perplexed wonder and no real understanding of how it was achieved. Yet there are snipe shots, brought up on its twisting and turning flight, who prove, simply by their contribution to the bag, that there is a little more to it than just luck. That they are more alert and prepared for instant action must offer a considerable advantage over those more used to the lengthy and noisy warning approach or slow lumbering rise (by comparison) of a pheasant.

The occasional snipe may appear on a pheasant drive, or the like, and, where it is unexpected, will often pass by unnoticed or unidentified. The majority are walked up in their own right, especially in the west and in Ireland where they are as important a quarry as the woodcock. Countless guns have argued over the correct way to walk up snipe. They will often sit quite tight amongst the cover in the bogs and marshes but, with the noise of the gun approaching downwind, they may flush too readily. Some feel, however, that a snipe, rising into wind, flashing its white belly, offers both a little more warning and time. Whichever method is practiced, the classic jinking flight will usually confuse and humiliate the gun. But such humiliation only serves to make us more determined.

There are a very few exceptional places where snipe are found in large enough numbers to warrant driven shooting. Drives may be from bogs, where the birds tend to flush singly or in small wisps, or from pasture, plough, winter cereals and turnip tops (where cattle have recently poached the ground). With little cover available, they will generally rise together – a dozen, perhaps, but sometimes a pack of 200 or more and the largest numbers tend to be found between the 400–600ft contours, except in hard weather when they move back to the bogs. Some fields traditionally hold good numbers of snipe whilst others, apparently similar, are ignored. The drives need to be checked a few days before to ensure the snipe are using them and, providing there is no change in the weather and the fields remain undisturbed, the birds should still be there. But they are unpredictable and a field which showed 200 snipe may be deserted only 3 days later.

There may be 12–14 drives in a day and, with such bustle, it is essential to understand whispered or hand-signalled instructions immediately for there is no time to question them. With guns, dogs and beaters at either end of a small field, there is a great risk that the snipe will be disturbed and the beaters simply have to trust that the guns are in place

*Drumming*

and start as soon as possible. There is a need for absolute silence and it is important that the guns do not stand out in the open for these birds are easily turned. Consequently one is often placed right up against a thick hedge, sometimes in a deep and restricting muddy ditch, where the only warning of approaching birds is a faint 'scaap' and a half-heard yell from the beaters, snatched away by the wind. Suddenly snipe seem to be calling from every direction as you desperately search up and down the line. Spinning round at a shot from your neighbour you realise a wisp of half a dozen must have passed low over your head and, in response to another shot, you turn again in exasperation to see a bird fall 20 yards behind. Sometimes they come over high, occasionally circling round again, higher still. A snipe 30–40 yards up makes a very small target and is remarkably easy to miss.

Watch and mark down your shot birds very carefully, including any lightly touched birds which set their wings. In a strong wind these 'floaters' can be carried a long way. Even dead birds can be remarkably difficult to pick. Good dogs are essential and they work best without the confusing scent of the gun's hopeless search with blundering and trampling footsteps.

## Jack Snipe (LYMNOCRYPTES MINIMUS)

FULLY PROTECTED IN GREAT BRITAIN, the jack snipe is still legal quarry in Ireland. It is found throughout the British Isles as a winter visitor, arriving in October and returning to its breeding grounds in Finland, the Baltic States and, to a lesser extent, Sweden in March. There has been a decline since the turn of the century but, though it may now possibly be stable, there is very little available information regarding its current status.

*Jack snipe*

The habits and habitat of the smaller jack snipe are very similar to the common snipe although, during its display flight, it makes a shallower dive. There is no drumming sound produced by the tail feathers and its display call is generally described as the sound of a distant galloping horse. In winter, it is usually encountered singly although it often shares the same habitat as the common snipe.

SEASON:
*Northern Ireland: September 1 – January 31*

Jack snipe are shot along with common snipe as incidentals and their protection in Great Britain gave rise to some concern as, in the excitement, the two little birds look very much alike. For those who encounter them regularly, they are as easily distinguished as woodpigeons and stock doves but most of us have had little chance to develop such a practiced eye

# *G*olden Plover *(PLUVIALIS APRICARIA)*

THE GOLDEN PLOVER IS found widespread throughout the British Isles in winter and, as a breeding species across Scotland, northern England (mostly the Pennines), parts of Wales, Exmoor, Dartmoor and north-west Ireland. Considerable numbers of winter visitors arrive in October from their breeding grounds in Iceland and Scandinavia, returning between February and April. Although increasing in Finland, it has been declining as a breeding species in the British Isles for some years. Increased afforestation and reduced moorland management are thought to be the cause of this decline.

In body size, the golden plover is marginally smaller than the woodcock but it is unlikely to be confused with any other bird on the quarry list. However, it does closely resemble the grey plover – a fully protected winter visitor. Sexes are alike and, in summer, the golden plover has a black face and underparts, bordered with white, and the crown and upperparts are spangled with black, brown and yellow. The grey plover, by comparison, appears to have more silvery upperparts. In the southern parts of its breeding range, the golden plover's face and underparts are less extensively black, for it breeds 2–3 weeks before the northern birds and the moult is arrested earlier. In winter, the belly becomes white, the face and chest are speckled with brown and the upperparts mottled and flecked with brown and buff. In flight, which is swift and direct, the axillaries are white rather than black, as in the grey plover, and it will sometimes obligingly raise its wings whilst standing to help with identification. Golden plover, in common with other plovers, have only 3 toes, completely lacking the hind toe. The call, a beautiful plaintive whistle, 'klui-wee', often gives their presence away although, with a high flying pack in the dusk, it can be quite ventriloquial and only a faint rush of wings indicates that they passed overhead.

Moulting between mid-March and mid-April, golden plover arrive in their moorland breeding grounds almost fully dressed in their stunning plumage. They are monogamous and territorial. The nest, a shallow scrape, lined with moss and other plant material, is usually well concealed amongst heather and the

clutch of, typically, 4 eggs is laid between April and June. Both parents share incubation and brood rearing duties, occasionally dividing the chicks and rearing them apart from each other. Nest predation is mostly by corvids, foxes, stoats and lesser black-backed and black-headed gulls, where there are nearby moorland breeding colonies, whilst adult golden plover are taken by foxes and peregrines. The young begin to fly at about 4 weeks and are independent a week or so later. Winter plumage is attained between mid-September and the end of October.

The golden plover's diet consists of insects, adult and larval beetles, earthworms, berries, seeds and grasses etc.. In winter, a great many are found on the coast as well as inland on old pasture and winter cereals, especially where

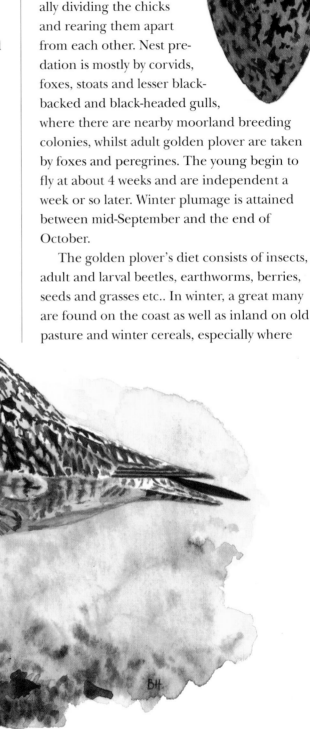

Summer

natural fertilizer is used. It is believed that many of the resident birds spend the winter in the lowland habitat adjacent to their breeding grounds and that the large concentrations found in the south-west are mostly winter visitors. Rarely seen singly at this time of year, flock sizes vary enormously and they are often encountered amongst flocks of lapwings,

although the two do not generally mix in flight. Golden plover are less subject to hard weather movements than lapwings and quickly return to their favoured feeding grounds after a thaw.

SEASON: *September 1 – January 31*

The golden plover makes a delicious meal and it is, perhaps, surprising that they are not a more important quarry. For some it is probably simply a case of not knowing what they are, whilst others make an active decision not to shoot them, much as some like to leave woodcock alone – a refreshing attitude.

Golden plover can be remarkably acrobatic in the air, especially after a shot has been fired. Indeed,

*Winter*

one method, occasionally practiced when the birds are too high, is to fire a shot in front of them. Often they will react by diving and, if the gun has reloaded quickly, provide a very fast and confusing flurry of targets.

They are generally very wary birds but can often be called within range by a gun imitating their soulful whistle and they have occasionally been stalked, the gun using the cover of a nonchalant cow, though it is not certain how readily these animals take directions.

# *C*urlew (NUMENIUS ARQUATA)

FULLY PROTECTED IN GREAT BRITAIN since 1981, the curlew is legal quarry only in Northern Ireland. It is found throughout the British Isles, though more commonly towards the north and west.

The curlew is our largest wader, although its curved bill accounts for a considerable amount of its length. The plumage is buff coloured, mottled and streaked with brown, with a white rump and barred tail. Curlew are only likely to be confused with the similarly shaped but smaller whimbrel which is a summer visitor to the north. However, the curlew lacks the broad dark stripes on the crown of its head, and its size and proportionately larger bill will usually distinguish the two. The call is a beautiful melancholy whistle: 'curl-ee'.

In the spring, curlew move inland to breed, favouring moors, heaths, bogs, marshes and upland meadows. Nests are generally sited in moderate or low vegetation, such as heather or grass, and the typical clutch of 4 eggs is laid between mid-April and May. Incubation and brood-rearing is carried out by both parents. The chicks, which have noticeable but uncurved bills, leave the nest shortly after hatching and begin to fly properly at about 5 weeks.

In mid-summer, curlew start to move back to their coastal haunts on the mudflats, estuaries and salt-marshes where their feeding habits are largely dictated by the tide. Probing the soft ground with their long bills, they feed mostly on the mudflats uncovered by the receding tide and their diet consists of molluscs, crustaceans, worms and other animal matter, though some vegetable material, such as seeds and berries, may be taken, especially inland. They are gregarious birds but, at low water, the feeding flocks can be fairly scattered. As the tide rises, they tend to gather on the sandbanks and when they are eventually pushed off they flight to inland fields.

SEASON:
*Northern Ireland: September 1 – January 31*
*Great Britain: fully protected*

Once an important quarry species on the foreshore in Great Britain, their fully protected status caused a certain amount of anger amongst wildfowlers. Although, as a table bird, it is generally considered to be at its best only in the early part of the season, it provided a square and welcome meal for those who could not afford to be so choosy.

Most curlew are shot either flighting inland on a making tide or returning to their feeding grounds on the ebb. In flocks, they are wary birds with keen eyesight and the gun needs to be well concealed.

# GEESE

## Greylag Goose (ANSER ANSER)

THE WILD GREYLAG IS, for the most part, a winter visitor to the British Isles, though a few hundred pairs remain to breed in the north of Scotland. There are increasing numbers of resident feral greylags, especially on the Norfolk Broads, which have descended from birds once released for shooting. About 100,000 wild greylags winter in Britain, representing a considerable increase over the last 50 years. However, there is thought to be a slight decline and over-shooting is believed to be the cause.

Although some are found on the east coast, the majority of greylags winter in Scotland and the north of England and are rarely seen in southern Ireland or the west country. The British wintering birds breed in the west of Iceland at a lower altitude than the pink-footed goose. In the spring the thaw comes earlier, enabling greylags to leave for their breeding grounds 10–14 days ahead of the pinks, whilst in the autumn the snows arrive later, allowing them to remain there for longer. There is also an eastern race which breeds in Scandinavia and Russia and winters on the continent.

Of the three grey geese on the British quarry list, the greylag is the largest and is the ancestor of most domestic geese. The sexes are alike and have a greyish-brown plumage with pink legs and a large orange bill (pink in the eastern race). The forewing is very pale and contrasts strongly with the rest of the plumage in flight. The call is a fairly coarse honking, similar to that of the domestic goose. Typically, skeins of geese, numbering up to 500 or more, fly in straggly, wavering v-formations, often with several, constantly changing peaks.

Greylags leave for their breeding grounds in April and immediately begin to claim their nesting sites. Whilst, in captivity, geese may not pair with the same bird the following year, it is generally believed that, in the wild, they pair for life, only taking another mate when the first has been killed. The nest itself is ill-concealed in short, rough vegetation, generally fairly close to water. A clutch of 5–6 eggs is laid in about May and incubated by the goose whilst the gander stands guard. Both parents aggressively defend the goslings which begin to graze from day one. For about 15–20 days during the moult, the adults become flightless and vulnerable to predation. The goslings make their first flights at 8 weeks but will not be fully mature and able to breed before their third year. Arctic foxes, together with gulls and skuas (both taking eggs and goslings), are the most important predators and gyrfalcons will also take adult greylags. In their winter range predation is minor, by foxes and peregrines.

Greylags return to the British Isles at the beginning of October and the family stays together, within a larger flock, throughout the winter. Roosting tends to be mostly on inland lochs and estuarine mudflats and sandbanks but they will also use wide rivers and large areas of floodwater. Flighting out at dawn to feed on stubbles, arable crops and old pasture, they return to the roost at dusk. In their breeding grounds, greylags ingest Icelandic lava as grit, to help grind up their food, and in winter, this is replaced by sand – usually found at the roosting site. Greylags will sometimes flight and feed under a moon, though to a lesser extent than other geese. Crop damage can sometimes be considerable but is often more to do with the puddling effects of a large flock than the amount they eat.

SEASON:
*September 1 – January 31 (extension in Great Britain only to February 20 in or over any area below the high water mark of an ordinary spring tide)*

Broadly speaking, although there is an overlap, wildfowlers can be split into two groups – goose hunters, who barely look at ducks, and duck hunters, who ignore geese – and neither consider inland shooting, be it geese coming into fields or duck into flight ponds, to be wildfowling. True wildfowling is a lonely game but, for those unbothered by discomfort, it is the most magical experience. There will be few shots but the rewards are in the sights, sounds and unpredictability. If you enjoy letting your gun off, go pheasant shooting.

Every morning, whatever the conditions, the geese flight from their roosts to their feeding grounds. They are extremely wary and the poorer the light, the easier it is for the gunner to remain undetected. As shooting pressure increases, they will often delay their departure, enabling them to see more as the light improves. Other than fog, a strong gale and a making tide provide the best chance for the gunner. In such conditions, they will be pushed off their roost and, if the water is too choppy for comfort, may lift off earlier. The closer in they are, the less distance they will have in which to gain height. If the gun is lucky, some may pass overhead and, if he is luckier still, the wind will be strong enough to keep them in range. At the evening flight, the gun intercepts the geese returning to their roosting grounds and may crouch in the same creek used for the morning flight, though facing in the opposite direction. Quite rightly, the actual roosting grounds are largely protected by wildfowling clubs.

The foreshore is a dangerous place for the careless gun and it is essential to know both the tides and which areas to avoid and to take a compass for it is easy to lose one's bearings in the darkness. Always take a dog – falling in water or across deep gullies, birds are often difficult to pick, especially in the fading light.

A rather more predictable way to shoot geese, though involving a certain amount of reconnaissance, is by calling and decoying into a well used field. Whilst it may not be

considered wildfowling, decoying does, at least, usually bring the birds within range and thus avoids the 'cowboy' shooting often encountered amongst a few bad guns, desperate to have a shot, on the foreshore. However, guns must not be tempted to make a large bag – that is, quite simply, not what goose shooting is about. Sadly, although the sale of dead geese is illegal, it has not stopped certain trigger-happy guns from overshooting. Most deplorable of all, however, is the use of rifles. A bird collapsing amongst a flock without a shot being heard, is a most unnerving experience for geese and they may desert a roosting or feeding ground for good. These beautiful birds deserve better.

Fortunately there are several big estates and reserves which do not allow geese to be shot and will always offer undisturbed feeding and roosting. Geese learn about them surprisingly quickly.

# Pink-footed Goose
## (ANSER BRACHYRHYNCHUS)

UNLIKE THE GREYLAG, the pinkfoot is totally migratory and winters in Britain as far south as the Wash and occasionally further. Their breeding grounds are in Spitsbergen, Iceland and north-east Greenland, the birds from Spitsbergen generally wintering in Denmark and Holland with the rest coming to Britain. In Iceland, their traditional breeding grounds are on the central plateau where the colder weather comes earlier and forces them to leave before the greylags. However, there is some evidence that the pinks are now beginning to move down into the river valleys to nest and that the two are starting to overlap. The pinkfoot population in Great Britain is about 230,000 and increasing every year.

*Pinkfoot*

Somewhat smaller than the greylag, the pinkfoot is rather prettier and more delicate. The plumage is also greyish-brown with white undertail coverts but the light grey forewing is not as pale as the greylag's. The bill is pink with a black base and nail and the legs are usually pink but may occasionally be yellow. In flight, the head and neck appear considerably darker than the body. Sometimes confused with the pinkfoot, the fully protected bean goose is generally larger, with a heavier, variable, black and orange bill and orange

*Pinkfoot*

legs. The pinkfoot's call, 'ang-ang' and 'wink-wink', is higher pitched than the bean's.

Pinkfeet begin the spring migration in late April – the last birds leaving in early May – and, as with the greylag, pairs are formed for life in their third year. Their diet in their breeding grounds consists of horsetail, cotton grass and other grasses, sedges and herbs. Nests are occasionally sited on cliffs but more usually on the ground and often on islands, amongst grass and are fairly visible. The clutch of 5–6 eggs is laid in May or June and both parents defend the brood. The goslings, grazing from the first day, are not dependent on insects but, nevertheless, grow quickly and begin to fly at 8 weeks. Arctic foxes and skuas are their most important predators.

The first arrivals reach Scotland in mid-September with the majority following towards the end of the month and into early October and dispersing about 4 weeks later. To the wildfowler, there are few more satisfying or spectacular sights. In order to lose height quickly, geese need to twist and spin sideways to spill the air from their wings. To see a large skein breaking acrobatically from their regimented flight formation, corkscrewing and whiffling down onto the sands, and to hear their magical chorus is an awe-inspiring and

breath-taking experience that leaves one feeling quite insignificant.

Although some pinkfeet roost on Scottish lochs, they are more of an estuarine goose. Like the greylag they are dependent on good agriculture and, around the new moon, their habits are similar – flighting inland to feed at dawn and returning at dusk. However, whilst most geese will travel about 5 miles to feed, the pinks may fly up to 20 miles or so to find undisturbed areas and they will flight under the moon more than any other goose. They are generally to be found on old pasture, stubbles or winter wheat and barley but will come into sugar beet tops and can cause considerable damage to carrots. In Scotland, some farmers will leave a few stubbles and old potato fields through the winter to keep the geese off their winter crops. Geese feed well whilst they are here and return to breed in good condition.

SEASON: *see greylag goose.*

During the period around a new moon, pinkfeet feed by day and rest by night and are generally shot by the same methods as greylags. However, the moon can have a considerable influence on their movements to the extent that, when it is full, they may feed at night and rest during the day. At other stages, there can be a mixture of day and night feeding, though generally they will not be found on the fields at night before the moon has risen or after it has set, except where there is a large amount of flood water. Providing there is background cloud cover, against which the birds can

*Bean goose –
fully protected*

be seen, the gun may have some very exciting shooting but there will be few nights during the season when the conditions are ideal.

*Pinkfoot*

# White-fronted Goose (ANSER ALBIFRONS)

THE EUROPEAN WHITEFRONT is thought to be the most numerous goose in the world, although only a fraction of the population winters in Britain – a few in Scotland but mostly on the Wash, river Severn, Kentish marshes and turning up almost anywhere on the south coast. However, the Greenland whitefront (*Anser Albifrons*

*Lesser whitefront - fully protected*

*flavirostris*), a largely protected sub-species – breeding, as its name implies, in Greenland – has a world population of only 28,000 or so, almost all of which winter in Ireland, Scotland, Islay and, occasionally, Wales. The breeding grounds of the European race are in the extreme north of Russia and Siberia.

The whitefront is much the same size as the pinkfoot with a similarly coloured plumage. However, they have orange legs, dark barring on the belly and, as their name suggests, white foreheads. The European race has an orange bill, with a white nail, whilst the Greenland's is larger and pink. Immature birds lack the white forehead and dark barring on the belly and, despite the orange legs, are easily confused with greylags. Confusion, however, is unlikely with the lesser whitefront, a rare, protected vagrant which is appreciably smaller, has a more exten- sive white foreheadand a yellow rimmed eye.

The European whitefront leaves for its breeding grounds in early March, some 4–6 weeks before the Greenland birds. Nesting in bogs on the Arctic tundra, their habits are similar to the other grey geese, with 5–6 eggs laid in May or June and the young, eating a predominantly grass diet, fly at about 8 weeks. Predation is by foxes, gulls and skuas.

The first European whitefronts can be expected to arrive any time from the begin- ning of October and the main lot follow in December as their wintering grounds in Europe freeze up. Greenland whitefronts

arrive on or around October 18. Whitefronts are mostly found on inland bogs, rushy meadows and marshes though some are encountered on estuaries. The main foods of the Greenland birds are the roots of the common cotton grass and the shoots of white beak sedge whilst the Europeans feed predominantly on grass and partly on winter cereals.

SEASON:
*Scotland and Northern Ireland: fully protected England and Wales: see greylag goose*

To avoid any confusion with the Greenland whitefront, the European is not allowed to be shot in Scotland – and very few winter there anyway. Otherwise, the shooting methods are similar to those used with greylags and pinkfeet.

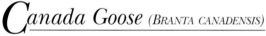

## *Canada Goose* (BRANTA CANADENSIS)

CANADA GEESE WERE INTRODUCED into private collections in Britain nearly 300 years ago and, gradually, escaped birds established themselves in the wild. Revered in North America, where it is a truly wild and migratory bird, the Canada goose in Great Britain is becoming a serious problem. Found on lakes in towns and cities, where control is almost impossible, and in the countryside, where their tameness often results in half-hearted, reluctant culls, their numbers are increasing dramatically.

The Canada has a greyish-brown body with paler underparts, a black rump and tail and white upper and undertail coverts. The neck and head is black with a broad white patch running from cheek to cheek under the throat. Sexes are alike though the gander is slightly larger. The call is a loud trumpeting honk. Barnacle and brent geese, similarly coloured and both fully protected, are very much smaller, with characteristic markings and are unlikely to be confused with the Canada.

Canada geese often start battling for nesting sites in February. Usually this is little more than a persistant chasing of rivals followed by a jubilant and triumphant return. Ultimately nests, on islands where possible, are often only about 15 yards apart and consist of a depression lined mostly with down.

Up to about 6 eggs are laid between March and May and incubated by the goose while the gander stands guard, though both will rear the

*Male stands guard at the nest*

brood. Survival is high with such attentive and aggressive parents and the young grow quickly on a predominantly grass diet, flying at about 8 weeks. Predation is minor though foxes will take adults given the opportunity.

The family party will stay together through the winter but usually join up with others to form big flocks on reservoirs and large lakes, feeding on the grassy banks or flighting out to farmland at varying times of the day to graze the winter crops.

SEASON: *see greylag goose*

In towns virtually the only way to control Canada geese is by piercing their eggs or replacing them with dummies. By the time the goose realises that nothing is going to hatch it will be too late to re-lay.

For the most part, in the country, Canada geese are remarkably tame, rarely bothering to leave lakeside banks for the safety of the water unless directly approached. In these circumstances it becomes very difficult to bring oneself to shoot them. Flushing them from water is almost impossible unless they have been shot regularly, but if they can be intercepted between the water and their

feeding grounds they prove to fly quite beautifully.

This is a very big bird with slow, deliberate wingbeats and it is important to remember that it looks to be a lot closer and slower than it really is. Note the distance of nearby trees to give an indication of range and aim for the head as though it were a small bird.

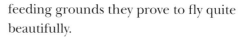

*Barnacle and brent for comparison - fully protected*

# DUCK

## *Mallard* (ANAS PLATYRHYNCHOS)

THE MALLARD IS the most common and widespread duck in the British Isles. Found on estuaries, coastal and inland marshes, lakes, ponds, rivers and, even occasionally, swimming pools, there are few areas of water shunned by this familiar bird.

The drake is instantly identified by the glossy green head, white ring at the base of the neck, dark brown chest, pale grey body and black coverts surrounding the white tail. A large yellow bill with a black nail, vivid orange legs and a blue speculum, bordered by black and white and usually only seen in flight, completes this smartly dressed bird. There are variations in the bill colour (sometimes a dull grey-green), the width of the neck ring and sometimes an almost total lack of the brown chest. Furthermore, there are various cross-bred plumage colours, from very dark brown to white. The duck, once commonly referred to as the wild duck, has a mottled dark and pale creamy brown plumage with a dark stripe through the eye and on the

crown. The bill is usually a dull orange broken with black and the legs a duller orange than the drake's. The duck's speculum feathers can often be seen at rest. The drake has a soft, almost purring quack, the duck a loud and confident one, often repeated insistantly. When flighting, even in quite small groups, they chatter together with a sound not dissimilar to the call of a magpie.

Mallard are surface feeders and sit quite high in the water with their tails up, unlike diving ducks whose tails slope down. They flush noisily, springing up from the water, unlike the divers which generally run along the surface.

However, the surface feeders can dive, albeit rather ungracefully, when washing and preening or avoiding danger. The legs of surface feeders are set towards the middle of the body enabling them to walk easily, if a little inelegantly, on land.

Mallard feed on water weeds and seeds, grain, insects and other aquatic animal matter, which, in water, they obtain by upending or dabbling on the surface.

Drakes can be seen displaying to the ducks at any time during the winter but increasingly towards the end of January. As winter comes to an end the mallard pairs can be found in more unusual places during the day – tiny streams, water-filled ditches, garden ponds barely two yards across and sometimes simply in the middle of fields – whilst the duck searches for a nesting site.

Nests are usually sited in thick vegetation often close to ponds and rivers but sometimes 200 yards or more from the nearest water source. Mallard will occasionally lay in a wide flat fork or large hole in a tree 10–15ft off the ground and such sites are often used every

year. The clutch of 7–15 white, buff or pale greenish-blue eggs are laid between February and May with later nests probably being the result of first nest predation – often significant in the early spring when there is little ground cover.

The drake makes only a token effort to defend the duck from the rape attempts of other drakes and plays no part in incubation or brood rearing though he is often nearby and may occasionally be seen with the family. As summer progresses, however, the drake becomes more reclusive, skulking in the reeds during the moult when he is flightless for about two weeks. In this eclipse plumage the drake is

sometimes mistaken for the duck, though darker and less clearly marked, and it may be as late as October or November before the full breeding plumage is attained once more.

The ducklings are reliant on chironomid midges and other aquatic insects for the first two weeks, gradually weaning themselves onto vegetable matter. Broods hatched in March struggle to find enough food, spreading out in their search and becoming easy targets for predators such as mink, pike, magpies, coots and moorhens(the latter two usually in defence of their own nests and young, though they have no qualms about taking eggs). Whilst predation is often the end result, cold wet weather which weakens the ducklings and affects the midge larval hatch is probably the real factor affecting their survival and it is not uncommon for a brood of 12 to be reduced to 1 or 2 in a matter of days.

The young can fly at about 7 weeks and by late August most family parties will be flighting in the evenings to feed on stubbles and ponds, generally resting up during the day on larger areas of water. This routine continues throughout the autumn and winter and ponds with a reliable natural or man-provided source of food become increasingly important. Mallard are often seen in pairs or small parties throughout the winter and it is assumed that these are generally family groups and that the pair bond remains quite strong outside the breeding season.

In the autumn large numbers of winter visitors arrive from northern Europe to swell the resident population.

*Duck with brood*

SEASON:
*September 1 – January 31 (extension in Great Britain only to February 20 in or over any area below the high water mark of an ordinary spring tide)*

Large numbers of mallard are reared and released for shooting every year. Often badly managed, over-fed and over-used to human presence, they rarely provide worthwhile shooting and more usually the performance can be likened to driving a chicken run.

Leaving aside driven duck – and this can be done with wild mallard though it is best not to disturb them on their day time resting ponds – most mallard will be shot flighting, to or from washes, marshes and the foreshore or to stubbles and flight ponds. Some ponds are naturally attractive to duck but many will only show the occasional pair and need to be fed to encourage a build up of numbers.

The evening flight generally begins shortly after sunset and continues until it is almost too dark to see –

*Drake*

normally a period of about 3/4 hour – and providing the pond is not shot more than 2 or 3 times during the season there is no harm in shooting through to the end of the flight. With man-fed ponds, a month or so between flights should allow plenty of time for the numbers to rebuild.

On wild and windy nights duck are often less cautious, being keen to come in without much circling, and shots fired on such a night will be whipped away, without warning the next party of approaching birds. However, it is always important to keep still and quiet and use your ears more than your eyes – a great white face searching the skies will be clearly visible.

When shooting in company, taking high circling duck will almost invariably mean that no one else gets a shot. Furthermore, it is not easy to judge distances in the half light and it is therefore more sensible to take your shot when the birds are within about 20 yards and committed to landing. Duck land into wind and this should be taken into account when deciding where to stand. Dogs are essential as wounded duck on the water are very hard to pick and dead duck in the dusk almost impossible to see. Above all the most important thing is safety. Other guns, even those nearby, quickly vanish in the gloom and, no matter what instructions are given at the outset, there is no guarantee that no one has moved.

Treat duck with the respect they deserve: do not over-shoot especially in hard weather – though many will move to the coast during long frozen spells – and continue to feed through to the spring. They provide very exciting shooting and it would be grossly unfair to stop feeding simply because the season is over. Game should always be well cared for in both open and closed seasons.

Stubbles can attract large numbers of mallard, especially early in the season. However, whilst a flight can build up on a pond almost anywhere, stubbles are, generally, only reliably productive in good duck country and a certain amount of reconnaissance is required to pin-point the favoured fields.

Pond and stubble flighting for duck should not be confused with wildfowling, which is discussed with wigeon. Flight ponds and stubbles usually offer a fairly comfortable and more predictable form of duck shooting, unknown to the true wildfowler.

*Upending*

# Wigeon *(ANAS PENELOPE)*

THE WIGEON IS THE staple quarry of the wildfowler and is predominantly a winter visitor, though about 500 pairs remain in Britain to breed – mostly in Scotland. Their main breeding grounds are in Iceland, Scandinavia, Russia and Siberia. Some 260,000 wigeon winter throughout Britain – especially on the Cambridgeshire washes, northern firths, Morecambe bay and along the North-umberland coast – and a further 100,000 visit Ireland. Both wintering and resident populations are increasing.

Rather smaller than the mallard, the cock wigeon is easily distinguished amongst other duck though, possibly, there may be some initial confusion with the drake pochard. The chestnut head, however, is crested with creamy-buff and the chest is pinkish rather than black. Furthermore, the wigeon is clearly a surface feeder, walking well on land and swimming with its fairly pointed tail held off the water. The speculum is dark green, bordered with black, and the white forewings and belly are very obvious in flight. The cock's call is a clear, sharp descending whistle – 'whee-oo'. The hen has a slightly reddish-brown plumage with white underparts and duller green speculum. In flight, wigeon form much tighter packs than mallard.

As the majority of wigeon leave for their breeding grounds in April, the resident pairs move to bogs and marshes to nest, though the site itself is often well away from water and,

typically, concealed amongst heather. The clutch of 5–10 eggs is laid in May and incubated by the hen only. The cock is often nearby but plays no part in nesting or brood rearing duties. The ducklings, eating mostly insects for the first 10–20 days and gradually becoming more vegetarian, are able to fly at about 6 weeks. In eclipse plumage, between June and October, the cock looks similar to, but darker than, the hen and both are flightless for about 2 weeks in July or August. The family probably holds together through the winter but loses its identity within the larger packs.

The majority of wigeon arrive at the end of September, though a few will usually appear at the beginning of the month, especially in the north. Wigeon are primarily a river and estuarine duck, though they will make use of large inland lakes and reservoirs, especially those with grassy banks. During the 1930s, disease hit the zostera, or eel grass, beds – at the time, their most important food. However, wigeon quickly adapted to a diet of grass and winter crops, unlike the brent goose which suffered a serious decline until it too discovered grazing and arable land. The brent was removed from the quarry list as a result and is still protected, though the population has probably now reached, and may even be in excess of, its original level. Prior to the disease, both birds were mostly encountered on the foreshore but they

can now be found almost anywhere. The beds have recovered in many places but, whilst wigeon still eat zostera, they no longer rely on it and the brent geese, in the south, often get to it first.

Resting on inland lakes or on the mudflats and sandbanks on the foreshore, wigeon can be active at any time of the day or night. They feed on the grassy banks of rivers and ponds and flight to flooded marshes or water flashes on winter wheat, barley, rape or closely grazed grass. They will also feed on wheat and barley stubbles, providing there is a water flash, but not to the same extent as mallard. However, where zostera is plentiful, wigeon may swim in and retreat with the tide, feeding as they go, and simply have no need to flight inland.

SEASON: *see mallard.*

Wildfowling clubs now largely control most of the foreshore areas suitable for ducks and geese, where shooting is allowed. They restrict the amount of disturbance by limiting the number of permits and, in some places, imposing bag limits.

For the shoulder gunner there are several ways to shoot wigeon and, indeed, other duck. As a rule, duck on the coast flight inland to feed at dusk and return to rest at dawn. Consequently the gun must either intercept them on the foreshore as they flight, or wait for them where they feed. With the geese flighting inland in the morning and returning at dusk, the gunner on the foreshore, interested in both, will need to look in opposite directions.

At the morning flight, when the returning duck are looking for quiet, sheltered roosting waters, they will be attracted to well-placed decoys. Anchored by a rope to the edge of a flooding gully, especially where signs show that duck have used the area before, it matters little that you may be trying to entice wigeon to

mallard decoys – they simply see what they believe to be ducks and, anyway, they will often mix when resting – even Canada goose decoys can work. Calling can be important, especially with mallard and wigeon flighting into feed at dusk, when decoys, disappearing in the gloom, have little effect.

When pushed off their roosts with a rising tide, duck tend to move about during the day and can provide some good shooting, though the flight will end at high tide. In rough weather, when the tide covers the mudflats, they can flight throughout the day to more sheltered inland water where decoys prove useful once more. Furthermore, duck will flight under a moon and, with a good cloud covering, the gun can shoot all night. Therefore, as with geese, the tides and weather conditions, especially the wind, are the important factors.

No account of wildfowling methods, however brief, would be complete without a mention of punt-gunning. Often likened to deer stalking, it is considered the finest sport in Britain. Limited to certain estuaries, there are thought to be 15–20 active punts each probably averaging about 6 outings a season and expecting to make one shot in 3 or 4. It requires enormous skill and knowledge to manoeuvre a punt to within 60–65 yards of a pack of duck without disturbing other birds and a considerable amount of cool judgement to refrain from shooting too soon. At the

*Hen*

## *Teal* (ANAS CRECCA)

A SMALL NUMBER OF resident teal are found in the British Isles but the majority migrate to breed in Iceland, Scandinavia, the Baltic States and Russia. Large numbers return in winter, particularly once the Dutch marshes have frozen up, and the main influx is in late December and January. Teal are possibly declining as a result of marsh drainage.

The teal is our smallest native duck and, arguably, the prettiest. Unlikely to be confused with any other duck, the cock teal has a chestnut coloured head with a broad green eyestripe, thinly edged with yellowish-buff. Upper parts and flanks are grey and the chest is buffish and liberally spotted with brown. A double line of black and white edges the scapulars and the speculum is green and black. The hen is similar to other female ducks, being a mottled brown and buff with a pale belly but both its size and green and black speculum should identify it. Teal rise lightly and effortlessly from the water and are

moment of truth, the gunner bangs the punt and fires as the birds open their wings. Whilst some shots are at geese, the punt-gunner is mostly after duck, especially wigeon and teal. Shooting only when they are well bunched ensures that most are killed cleanly and, with skill and luck, he may pick up a dozen or so.

*Cock wigeon*

remarkably agile and acrobatic in the air, especially in packs.

Teal breed throughout the British Isles, though to a lesser extent in the south. The nest is sited in dense ground cover, often in a wooded or moorland habitat but generally close to water, and a clutch of 7–9 eggs is laid in May. The cock plays no part in incubation or brood rearing and assumes eclipse plumage between July and October, appearing similar to the hen but darker. As with other ducks, the

*Eclipse plumage coming through*

*Cock*

adults become flightless for about 2 weeks during the moult – the males before the females – and with the teal, this occurs in August. Insects are crucial for these little ducklings during the first 14 days but they grow fast and are able to fly at 4–5 weeks. Due to their small size, adult teal are probably more vulnerable to predation by hawks and falcons than any other duck.

Outside the breeding season, teal can be found in almost any watery habitat –

rivers, ponds, lakes, bogs, marshes or on the fore-shore. They are quiet, secretive birds and prefer peaceful and secluded resting ponds edged with thick cover. Mallard and teal share a similar habitat although, with a diet of water weeds, seeds, grain and invertebrates, the little teal is dependent on very shallow water for feeding. Possibly because they do not much care for the mallard's boisterous and greedy nature, suitable ponds will generally show one or the other but rarely both in good numbers.

SEASON: *see mallard.*

In the gloom of dusk, a gentle 'pfft' of wings and the smallest ripple on the pond's surface is often the only indication that a pair of teal have arrived. The steam train rush of a circling pack

*Hen*

provides more warning but they still come in with remarkable speed and agility. At the sound of a shot, they sit on their tails and rocket skywards, when the combination of poor light and their small size may convince one that they are out of range within a fleeting moment.

A spring of teal may sometimes appear on a pheasant drive from boggy woodland and they will often sit tight amongst the rushy edges of ponds, allowing the gun to walk them up during the day but they are generally shot by the same methods as mallard and wigeon.

# Pintail (ANAS ACUTA)

LARGELY MIGRATORY, THE PINTAIL'S main breeding grounds are in central and northern Russia, the Baltic States, Scandinavia and Iceland. A few remain in East Anglia but most of the small resident population breed in Scotland. Generally preferring certain coastal

*Drake*

areas, pintail can be found almost throughout the British Isles once the migrants arrive in October and November but the majority winter on the Ouse washes. The population is increasing.

If the teal is the prettiest duck, the pintail must be the most graceful and elegant. Although more slender, it is a longer bird than the mallard. The drake is unmistakable with its long, sharply pointed tail, chocolate-brown head and white throat, chest and underparts. The speculum is bronze and green and edged with buff and white. The duck has a mottled brown and buff plumage with a duller speculum and shorter tail than the drake. However, the tail is clearly more pointed than that of the gadwall, with which it is most easily confused, and the speculum provides a positive identifi-cation amongst all species.

Pintail nest near lakes, ponds, bogs or marshes – the migratory birds leaving for their breeding grounds in April. About 9 eggs are laid in May-June, usually amongst low scrub, though sometimes rather poorly concealed, and the duck carries out incubation and brood-rearing duties alone. The ducklings are dependent on an insect diet for the first 10–14 days, gradually becoming more vegetarian, and begin to fly at about 5–6 weeks. Adult drakes are in eclipse between July and October and are flightless for about 2 weeks in August, a short while before the

*Duck and drake*

ducks. Nest and duckling predation by corvids, gulls and foxes can be significant but the enemies of adults are few.

During the winter, the pintail's diet consists of water weeds, seeds and grain (from stubbles and ponds) and, in their estuarine habitat, a considerable amount of animal material (molluscs and other invertebrates) is eaten. Having longer necks than other ducks, pintail are able to feed in deeper water.

SEASON: *see mallard.*

Pintail are locally important as a quarry species but most guns will probably only shoot them as incidentals on the foreshore or nearby ponds etc., whilst flighting other duck.

# Shoveler *(SPATULA CLYPEATA)*

THE SHOVELER IS LARGELY a winter visitor, arriving in September and leaving in about April, and is found across most of the British Isles. There is a small resident breeding population but the majority of the British wintering birds breed in Scandinavia and the Baltic States and a few in eastern Iceland.

With its very long, broad and spatulate bill, the shoveler cannot really be confused with any other bird although, where it is unexpected, the drake may be dismissed as a mallard, purely on the basis of its green head. The shoveler, however, is slightly smaller and has a strikingly white chest, contrasting with its chestnut-brown flanks and belly, and both ducks and drakes have pale blue forewings and green speculums.

The shoveler's well concealed nest is found in boggy, marshy areas, more commonly amongst long grassy vegetation than reeds, and close to water. The 8–12 eggs are sometimes laid in late April but mostly in May, and incubation and brood-rearing is carried out by the duck alone. Drakes are in eclipse between May and November and become flightless, before the ducks, for about 2 weeks in July. The ducklings are dependent on insects for the first 14 days or so and begin to fly at 6–7 weeks.

Shoveler are usually encountered in small groups in winter, sometimes consisting only of drakes, and their habits become similar to the other duck species. Living on a diet of invertebrates and vegetable matter, they rarely up-end and are, thus, dependent on the muddy shallows where they sift the food-rich water as they swim. They are often found resting on old gravel pits and lakes during the day but the marshes and flooded areas where they feed are susceptible to freezing and they readily move to the foreshore as a result. Marsh drainage may be affecting the shoveler although they are generally thought to be increasing.

SEASON: *see mallard.*

Shoveler are shot by the same methods as other duck. However, with the considerable amount of animal content in their diet, they are not generally considered to be a great delicacy. If the gun is not prepared to eat them, they should be left alone.

*Feeding*

Pintail

Duck shoveler

Shoveler

Drake shoveler

Drake pintail

# Gadwall (ANAS STREPERA)

THE GADWALL WAS UNKNOWN as a breeding species in the British Isles prior to its introduction into Norfolk in the mid 19th century. Although widespread, gadwall are rather uncommon across their European range and the majority of our wintering birds are home bred – mostly in East Anglia – though a few arrive from Iceland, Scandinavia and, possibly, central Europe. The population is increasing.

From a distance, gadwall are probably the hardest of all the British duck to identify. The drake is neither colourful nor strongly marked but appears quite grey with a black bill, darkly marked chest and black undertail coverts. The duck is a mottled brown and buff, easily confused with the somewhat larger duck mallard although the belly is white. Not always seen when the bird is at rest, it is the white speculum, separated from a maroon wing patch by a black bar, which provides positive identification.

The gadwall's nest is sited close to the water, in the thick, marginal, reedy vegetation of lakes and ponds and a clutch of 8–12 eggs is laid in May or June. Incubation and brood-rearing is carried out by the duck alone and the ducklings, dependent on insects for the first 10–14 days, start to

Drake gadwall

*Gadwall pair*

This handsome diving duck is often seen on lakes in towns and cities. Easily identified, being slightly larger than the tufted and mid-way between the teal and mallard, the drake has a red eye, rich chestnut head and neck, black chest, pale grey body and black tail area. The duck is a soft, slightly reddish-brown with a paler area around the bill and throat. Their heads have a triangular profile and, on water, they have the classic, tail down, diving duck shape. Like the tufted, they are only occasionally seen on land and take off by running along the water surface. In flight, their wings are quite grey and the wingbar is paler but not

fly at 6–7 weeks. Drakes are in eclipse between June and September and both adults become flightless for about two weeks in August.

During the winter, gadwall are generally found on inland lakes, rivers and reservoirs but occasionally, and perhaps increasingly, on the coast. Usually encountered in pairs or small groups, possibly family parties, their habits are similar to most other duck – resting by day and flighting to shallower water, to feed on water weeds, seeds and some animal matter, at dusk.

SEASON: *see mallard.*

Gadwall are generally flighted into ponds and lakes in the evenings. Most are probably shot as odd incidentals but some ponds, either regularly or temporarily, seem to almost exclusively attract gadwall, though rarely in very large numbers.

*Gadwall*

## Pochard (AYTHYA FERINA)

ALTHOUGH THERE IS A very small resident population of 200–400 pairs, the pochard is largely a winter visitor to the British Isles with up to 50,000 birds arriving in October and November from their main breeding grounds in Scandinavia, the Baltic States and Russia. The population is increasing.

*Drake pochard*

*Duck pochard*

*Tufted*

*Pochard*

*Goldeneye*

white, as in the tufted. In the hand, they have a stocky appearance, the wings seeming too small for flight to be possible.

For nesting, pochard require lakes with thick marginal sedges and reedbeds. The nest is a fairly large, raised construction built up out of reeds and other vegetation, well concealed and very close to the water's edge. The clutch of 6–8 eggs is laid in April or May and incubation and brood-rearing is carried out by the duck alone. The drake assumes eclipse plumage from July to October and becomes flightless for about 2 weeks during August, a short while before the duck. The ducklings, unlike those of the tufted, are yellow and brown. However, as they rarely stray from their mother and dive readily around her, they are unlikely to be confused with mallard ducklings. The divers are less dependent on good weather to provide a rich source of animal foods than the surface feeders and they quickly feather up, though they do not fly until 7–8 weeks. Predation is not usually a major problem as they are generally close enough to their mother to be defended by her and, consequently, although the broods can be small, duckling survival is often high, especially with the tufted duck.

As winter approaches, pochard move to larger lakes, gravel pits and reservoirs, gathering in considerable flocks as the migrants arrive and only moving to the coast in very hard weather. The ducks tend to winter further south than the drakes which explains why such flocks often show an imbalance between the sexes. Whilst they are frequently seen on the same lakes, pochard prefer shallower water to tufted duck and their diet is more vegetarian outside the breeding season. Like all duck, they will make use of grain on flight ponds.

SEASON: *see mallard.*

As with the other divers, the pochard is not avidly pursued like the surface feeders. However it does make very good eating and is a welcome addition to the bag.

# Tufted Duck (AYTHYA FULIGULA)

THE TUFTED DUCK WAS once a rare breeding species in the British Isles but there is now a modest resident population of several thousand pairs. Their main breeding grounds, however, are in Iceland, Scandinavia, the Baltic States and eastwards through Russia and Siberia and very large numbers arrive in the British Isles in September and October to spend the winter. Both the resident and wintering populations are increasing.

A familiar diving duck on both urban and country lakes, the tufted is only likely to be confused with the similar, but almost totally migratory and coastal, scaup. The tufted drake, however, has a dark brown back and purplish-black head with the long, diagnostic tuft. The chest and undertail coverts are black, leaving the flanks and belly white. The scaup, by comparison, has a grey back and greenish tuftless head. Females are more easily confused, both being a darkish brown with paler flanks and white underparts, but a combination of habitat and the small head tuft should identify the duck tufted. The scaup has a considerable amount of white around the base of the bill which, in the tufted, is variable, but generally not as large and sometimes lacking.

Tufted have white wingbars, replacing the colourful speculums of the surface-feeders and contrasting with the dark upper parts. They are unable to rise straight from water, instead needing to run along the surface, but once airborne they are strong, fast fliers. Rarely seen more than a few feet from the edge of water, they are ungainly on land and have an upright, uncomfortable stance.

In late winter tufted are often found on smaller lakes, seeking out possible nesting sites but a considerable amount of time elapses between the pair's apparent decision to stay and the disappearance of the duck to nest. The clutch of 5–8 eggs, laid in late May or June, is usually well concealed in thick reeds or other ground vegetation close to the water's edge. The drake plays no part in incubation or brood-rearing duties, often disappearing

*Drake*

shortly after the eggs hatch, and is in eclipse between July and November when it is hard to tell the sexes apart. The drake becomes flightless for about 2 weeks in August or September, a short while before the duck. The brown ducklings, able to dive for food from day one, are dependent on a diet of chironomid larvae, and crustaceans etc. for about 14 days, gradually increasing the vegetable content, and are able to fly at 7–8 weeks.

Outside the breeding season, tufted tend to gather in considerable numbers on large lakes, gravel pits and reservoirs, resorting to rivers and ultimately the foreshore during a big freeze. Requiring a running take-off, they avoid small areas of water surrounded by trees but will flight to more open ponds to feed on grain, aquatic vegetation and invertebrates – almost exclusively obtained by diving. However, their daytime resting water may well provide them with enough food without the need to look elsewhere. Whilst they feed sporadically throughout the day, amid periods of rest, they generally become more active at dusk.

SEASON: *see mallard.*

*Duck*

Shot on ponds and lakes, tufted are small, quick and easily missed and if they were as good to eat as the surface feeders, they would no doubt be a more important quarry species. Nevertheless, they are far from inedible and many are shot as a result.

*Duck*

# *S*caup *(AYTHYA MARILA)*

IT IS MOST IMPORTANT to point out, firstly, that scaup are legal quarry only in Northern Ireland.

Scaup are winter visitors to the British Isles, though some occasionally breed in the north of Scotland. They arrive from their breeding grounds in Iceland and Scandinavia in late September-October, with those from Russia and Siberia wintering on the continent. They are more coastal than the other divers on the quarry list with large concentrations being found on the Firth of Forth in particular.

The scaup can easily be confused with the slightly smaller tufted duck, although they are often separated by a different habitat. The drake scaup has a greenish-black head together with a black breast and tail. The back is grey and the flanks and underparts are white. The duck is very similar to the tufted, being darkish brown with paler flanks and a white belly, but there is a large amount of white on the face at the base of the bill – less conspicuous or missing in the tufted. Scaup do not have a tuft on the head.

The pairs usually form before the birds leave for their breeding grounds in March-April, although the females tend to winter further south than the males. Pressure on suitable sites near ponds, lakes and rivers can sometimes lead to nests being found close together, though scaup do not form breeding colonies. The nest itself is usually hidden amongst tussocky grass, close to the water, and a clutch of 7–11 eggs is laid in May-June. Incubation and brood-rearing is carried out by the duck alone. The ducklings swim and dive for food from the first day and begin to fly by about 6–7 weeks. Drakes are in eclipse between July and November and are flightless for about 2 weeks in August or September, a short while before the ducks.

In their winter range, scaup can be found

*Drake*

on gravel pits and lakes but they are seldom encountered far inland and tend to favour estuaries and shallow coastal inlets. Their diet consists mostly of animal matter such as crustaceans, insects, mussels and other molluscs which is almost exclusively obtained by diving. However, like most ducks, scaup will also take advantage of grain when available.

SEASON:
*Northern Ireland: September 1 – January 31*
*Great Britain: fully protected*

As a table bird, despite the considerable amount of animal material in their diet, some people consider scaup make fairly good eating and liken them to tufted. Those who are not prepared to eat them should leave them alone.

# Goldeneye (BUCEPHALA CLANGULA)

THE GOLDENEYE HAS ONLY bred in the British Isles since the early 1970s and, whilst it has become a fairly common breeding bird in Invernessshire, it rarely nests to the south and the birds there represent almost the total resident population. The majority are winter visitors, arriving in October from their breeding grounds in Scandinavia and the Baltic States – birds breeding further east probably remaining on the continent. Both residents and migrants are increasing.

The goldeneye's very distinctive markings and swollen-headed appearance allow for easy identification. The bill is more goose-like than other ducks' and the drake has a dark green head, yellow eye and a large white facial spot. A black back provides a strong contrast with the white chest, flanks and underparts. The duck has a dark chestnut-brown head, white collar, and greyish-brown body. Occasionally the yellowish-ochre area near the tip of her bill is lost after the breeding season whilst the

*Goldeneye pair*

drake's remains black throughout the year. Unlike other divers, goldeneye can rise directly into the air and, whilst flying, their wings produce a loud whistle. The white wing patches are strikingly highlighted by the dark primaries in flight.

Courtship begins before the birds leave for their breeding grounds in about April, the drakes throwing their heads back with their bills pointing up in the air. The nest is sited in a tree hole or nest box and the clutch of 6–8 eggs is laid in May or June. Larger clutches are probably the result of dump-nesting by more than one duck – occurring under nest site pressure. The drake, playing no part in parental duties, assumes eclipse plumage between August and November and becomes flightless for about 2 weeks in September, a short while before the duck. Tumbling to the ground, often from a considerable height, the white-cheeked ducklings quickly learn to dive for food (mostly animal matter) and are able to fly by 7–8 weeks.

As winter approaches, the golden-eye's summer diet of larvae, molluscs and fish changes to worms, mussels, crustaceans and grain. They are

*Drake displaying*

usually encountered as single birds or in small flocks on lakes, gravel pits and reservoirs but they are also coastal birds, unlike tufted and pochard, and are often found on estuaries.

SEASON: *see mallard.*

Due to the minimal amount of vegetable matter in their diet, the goldeneye is generally considered to be pretty inedible. Unless the gun is prepared to eat them, they should be left alone.

# PIGEONS AND DOVES

## Woodpigeon (COLUMBA PALUMBUS)

THE WOODPIGEON, PIGEON or ring dove, is found in varying numbers throughout the British Isles but is generally increasing again after a decline in the 1960s and '70s. This increase is thought to be due to the large areas of oil seed rape now being grown which provide an ample supply of food throughout the winter.

The pigeon cannot really be confused with any other bird, though both stock doves and sparrowhawks are frequently mistaken for pigeons. Both of these are fully protected birds and, fortunately, the mistake is usually realised before a shot is fired. Stock doves are quite common in Great Britain and frequently seen when shooting pigeons and it is, therefore, important to note the differences. Woodpigeons are larger and have white collars and wing bars and a pinker chest. Whilst pigeons generally have even flowing wingbeats, the stock dove's are more pronounced and the neck seems shorter. However, everyone sees flight patterns differently and there is no substitute for simply studying them in the field.

The pigeon makes display flights in the spring with a series of steeply rising and descending undulations, clapping wings at the peaks, and often returning to the tree where the flight began. The nest, made of twigs, is a fairly flat, uncomfortable looking platform in a tree, bush or amongst ivy and is often poorly hidden. The two white eggs are clearly visible from above and nest predation is high. However, it is quite common to see pigeons incubating in October and, with such a long breeding season, two or three broods are possible. The young squabs, cared for by both parents, are fed on pigeon milk, which is regurgitated from the adult's crop, and leave the nest after about 3–4 weeks but they remain dependent on their parents for food for a short while. Immature pigeons lack the white collar but the wing bars will tell them apart from stock doves. Flight feathers are usually moulted in sequence, allowing pigeons to continue to fly normally, but very occasionally the odd bird may lose too many at once and become flightless. The majority of these will fall prey to foxes, cats and stoats etc – not otherwise major enemies of the pigeon. Sparrowhawks will also occasionally take pigeons but perhaps the most spectacular predator is the peregrine.

The autumn provides the pigeon with an abundance of food: grain on the stubbles and newly drilled fields as well as berries, beech mast, acorns and other seeds. As winter progresses, rape becomes increasingly important as it is easily accessible, even in moderate snow. However, rape is of poor nutritional value and large amounts need to be consumed every day, explaining the vast array of scaring devices set out by the farmers. Large numbers of migrants arrive from the continent in winter and damage to crops can be severe. It is only when the snow is deep enough to cover the rape for more than a week or two that the pigeons suffer for there is little else for them other than ivy berries or maize and kale in game cover strips. Mild winters ensure a high survival rate.

Effectively there is no close season for pigeons – various open general licences having been granted, in respect of the pest species of birds, to guns in Great Britain in 1992 by both the Department of Environment and the Ministry of Agriculture, Fisheries and Food, after a worrying time when seasons seemed almost inevitable.

To the shooting man or woman the pigeon cannot be considered a pest. It offers the most superb variety of shots. Its agility in the air can change a straightforward shot in an instant. Irate farmers call it many things but, perhaps, 'the poor man's grouse' best sums up this bird. However, whilst it certainly does not command the vast amounts of money that grouse shooting does, it is rarely the free shooting it once was. Indeed some people earn their living by taking clients pigeon shooting.

*Tail feather – underside*

A large proportion of pigeons are shot over decoys. Decoying is a calculated art form. Those who are successful spend a great deal of time watching pigeons. They know which crops to study; where best to set up a hide; how to arrange an enticing and natural looking pattern of decoys; where the pigeons rest, in between bouts of feeding, and when they are active.

Whilst they proved successful for many years, the older decoys with their heads up and large white splashes on their necks are thought by some to actually warn pigeons of danger and the more common decoys in use nowadays are of the head down and feeding type. However, shot pigeons set up in the field provide the most effective decoys. Cradles and flapping machines simulate birds coming into land and the sort of technology found in coarse fishing will, no doubt, be commonplace in a few years.

Pigeons landing into wind amongst decoys will present very similar targets and a well constructed hide will mean the gun is unlikely to be seen, keeping the twisting, evasive action to a minimum. There is not a lot of mark-up on the price of a cartridge in pigeons sold at the game dealer and the 'professional' needs to shoot straight, pleasing the farmer in the

*Squab*

process, and cannot therefore waste his time shooting at high passing or circling pigeons. He will have already marked out, in his mind, the most effective area in which to take a shot and his decoy pattern will unerringly draw the pigeons to that spot.

Perhaps the most exciting form of pigeon shooting is the evening flight. With the young fully-fledged, the pigeons return to their habit of roosting together in favoured woods and this can be in very large numbers once the winter migrants arrive. Pigeon flighting becomes possible once the leaves fall from the trees, although most pheasant shoots will not tolerate such disturbance in their woods until after the season and generally this February shooting will be offered to those who have helped out over the past year. On the rough shoot, where the pigeon is as important as the pheasant, flighting can be done when the conditions are right regardless of whether it disturbs other game and it is probably fair to say that a shot fired in February, in a wood that has been driven several times during the season, is more likely to upset the pheasants than a barrage of shots in November on a rough shoot, despite the former having hand reared pheasants and the latter wild. Pigeons can be quite choosy and tend to avoid exposed, draughty woods although those that

seem favourable may not always be so. As with decoying, watching their movements will confirm which woods are being used as will the amount of fresh droppings found under the trees.

Gales will always make the most exciting shooting. Whilst birds coming into the trees in a small spinney can often be covered by a single gun, in large woods on a still evening they will come over too high except for those landing in trees immediately around the gun. In strong winds the birds will be lower and the well positioned gun should get plenty of shooting, from about an hour before sunset, and the sound of the shots will be whipped away without disturbing too many approaching birds.

Generally the woods will be gloomy enough at that time of day and it should not be necessary to conceal oneself too carefully. However, pigeons twisting and side-slipping over the tops of the trees will rarely provide straightforward shots and it is important to ignore the trees rather than try to shoot through any gaps in the branches. The birds will be approaching into wind which gives one the advantage of at least knowing which

## Collared Dove (STREPTOPELIA DECAOCTO)

UNKNOWN IN GREAT BRITAIN prior to the 1950s, the collared dove has spread rapidly throughout the British Isles and is a common sight in parks and gardens as well as in the countryside, especially around farm buildings.

Considerably smaller than the woodpigeon, the collared dove is only likely to be confused with the turtle dove which is a summer visitor and fully protected. The collared dove is a pale buff colour with a black collar, edged with white, and has a fairly square ended tail which is dark underneath and tipped with a broad white band. The turtle dove appears much darker and the tail, edged with white, is more pointed. In flight the collared dove appears less delicate and the wings and tail less pointed. The turtle dove has a purring call compared with the collared dove's triple 'coo' and a call, made in flight during the breeding season, similar to the sound made by paper and a comb.

The collared dove's breeding habits are similar to the pigeon's and numbers can reach excessive levels locally, especially where food, put out for other birds and livestock, is easily accessible.

SEASON:
*Great Britain: there is effectively no close season –*
*see woodpigeon*
*Northern Ireland: protected*

Shooting can provide an effective control on numbers due to the bird's habit of concentrating in a relatively small area. Such collared dove populations are usually quite tame, unless shot

direction to face, although it is always worth an occasional look behind, especially when someone else has fired and, in a gale, such hurtling downwind pigeons will test the reactions of the best shots. The bags will rarely be large but the shooting will be very exciting with an infinite variety of shots.

Pigeons often use well defined flightlines between their feeding and resting areas, perhaps along a hedge or belt of trees. Where the gun is unable to cover the width of their path, a decoy, lofted into a tree, may bring them within range and this can also work when roost shooting or, during the afternoon in early autumn, as the birds come back to rest in between bouts of feeding. At other times they will be shot as extras, clattering out of trees when rough shooting or on driven shoots – though in the case of partridge shooting this will often be frowned upon.

It is arguable whether pigeon shooting offers an effective control on numbers but, at the very least, it keeps them off the crops at critical times (or minimises the damage by moving them on) and the vast numbers that are shot each year probably keeps the population healthy.

frequently, in which case, as they become wilder, they are less likely to tolerate the human activity around the farm buildings and most will move to a non-shooting neighbour.

# Feral Pigeon (COLUMBA LIVIA)

FERAL PIGEONS CAN BE found throughout the British Isles – mostly in towns and cities and the immediate surrounding countryside.

Descended from rock doves, they were originally tame escapees from dovecotes and adapted to a semi-domesticated life in the wild. Cross-breeding with escaped racing pigeons has produced a wide range of plumage variations.

Even without the food deliberately offered them, they survive on the farmer's crops and by general scavenging and perhaps without them to clean up after us something less acceptable would take their place.

There is effectively no close season (see woodpigeon) but, whilst feral pigeons can cause considerable mess and damage to buildings and crops, the very fact that their habits and habitat are so closely linked to man makes them impossible to control by shooting.

# CORVIDS

# Magpie (PICA PICA)

THE MAGPIE CAN BE found throughout most of the British Isles from city gardens to farmland and parkland. It is a corvid, a member of the crow family, and inherits their very wary, cautious nature especially in the countryside.

Unless very close, the magpie appears to be black and white with both sexes alike. The head, neck, chest and back are black as is the large and powerful beak. The tail is long and irridescent and the underparts are white with black legs. The primaries are white with black edging and between these and the large white area of scapular feathers the rest of the wing is irridescent.

The magpie has a fairly upright stance tending to bounce along the ground as opposed to walking. In flight the long tail and rounded wings are most noticeable. Flight itself is faltering with hurried flapping, often broken by short swooping glides, and the bird appears to make rather slow progress. The call is a harsh, often repeated, chatter, similar to a football supporter's rattle.

Magpies start building new or repatching old nests in late winter. They are territorial in spring and early summer, aggressively defending their territory from other magpies. The nest is hard to ignore when there are no leaves on the trees, being a very large construction of twigs like a ball and often larger than squirrels' dreys – the latter appearing to be more like a ball of leaves. The nest is roofed, which explains its size, and is usually found in quite thick medium sized trees, such as blackthorn, and dense hedgrows but sometimes in tall trees, like alders, almost right at the top. A clutch of 4–8 eggs is laid in April or early May and the chicks, fed by both parents, leave the nest at about 3–4 weeks. As winter approaches, magpies can form large foraging and roosting flocks. Whilst there are no major predators, sparrowhawks will occasionally take them.

Magpies are opportunists and have an extremely varied diet of grain, berries, fruit, insects, eggs, young birds and carrion. Whilst they will rob nests of young and have actually been seen taking ducklings from water, one must assume that, in the case of gamebirds, whose chicks leave the nest shortly after hatching, the parents can usually provide some protection for the young. Where magpies really cause the damage to game (and are particularly successful in doing so) is in egg predation.

THERE IS EFFECTIVELY NO CLOSE SEASON:
*see woodpigeon.*

The magpie has increased greatly in numbers since the war, due primarily to the decline of gamekeepers and the banning of the use of poisons. Their cunning and wariness has meant that their success has gone practically unchallenged by all but the most dedicated vermin controllers. Jays are also quite wary but many are shot on driven pheasant days. Not so the magpie, which seems to have a remarkable ability to find the only escape route from a covert.

The advent of the Larsen trap has meant that shooting magpies has become a fairly pointless and time-consuming way of reducing their numbers. The only reason that their numbers need to be controlled is because of their predation of eggs and young birds (not just game-birds). It is therefore not necessary to control them outside the breeding season as they are not then doing any harm and, anyway, others will simply come in to replace them in the spring.

It is believed that territorial magpies cause considerably more damage than the non-territorial birds. The Larsen trap holds a live decoy bird (which must be properly fed and watered and a shelter provided) and is introduced into each territory, catching each territorial pair in turn. Even if you have not made a note of where the nests are before the leaves open it is relatively easy to pin-point a territory by the amount of magpie activity you see and hear.

Without a Larsen trap you have a job on your hands as they are not stupid birds. Flush the magpie from its nest and you may have a very long wait before it returns, and then only if you have kept still and well hidden. The best chance is to shoot before it enters the nest as the mass of twigs offers considerable protection from shot.

Leaving a rabbit or some eggs in a quiet field corner, frequented by magpies, can also work but there may be an hour or so to wait and even when they find the bait they may be too suspicious to commit themselves immediately. A rifle will enable you to withdraw from the area, lessening the risk of being seen.

Waiting in a hedgerow well used by magpies can prove successful but, often as not, the birds will see you approach, leave perhaps the very tree you have decided to wait beneath and will probably watch you from a distance and boycott the hedge for a few hours.

It is possible to get to within about 100 yards of them by walking in the open and a good rifle shot may fare well with this method but a missed shot might make them reluctant to allow you that close again. Whilst they may not fly off altogether in such circumstances they will rarely stay on the ground, preferring to fly up into a hedge or tree. The angle of such a shot with a rifle, even at quite moderate ranges can make it a particularly dangerous one.

Presumably due to their being partial to eating road casualties, magpies are extremely trusting of vehicles even where they do not normally see them and it is quite often possible to get within shotgun range. However, even with the engine turned off, this could be construed as pursuing winged quarry with the aid of a motor vehicle which is against the law.

The only other chances at magpies will be when least expected, not having deliberately set out for them in the first place and they will be rare.

Verdict:
Get a Larsen trap and forget about shooting magpies.

## Jay (GARRULUS GLANDARIUS)

THE JAY, ANOTHER CORVID, is common and widespread throughout most of the British Isles except in the north of Scotland and north and west of Ireland.

Almost impossible to confuse with any other bird, the jay has a pinkish-brown plumage with a dark tail and streaked crest. In flight the white rump and brilliant blue flash of its wing coverts allow for easy identification. When alarmed, the jay will often advertise its presence with a screeching call.

The nest – considerably smaller than the magpie's – is sited in a bush or tree, rarely high up, and the 4–6 eggs are laid in April or May. Both parents help to rear the brood and the family party can often still be seen together in early autumn.

Broadleaved woodland is the favoured haunt of the jay and they will rarely be found far from trees. They are constantly on the move, whether on the ground or in a tree, and this activity is most noticeable in the autumn when they are busy amongst the oaks, finding and burying acorns to tide them through the winter. Thus, both jays and squirrels benefit from the trees their ancestors planted as acorns and forgot. Apart from the prominence of acorns, their diet is similar to the other corvids but the jay is not as black as it is painted. Egg predation is minor but a few

*Wing covert feather*

rogues can wreak havoc amongst song bird nestlings.

THERE IS EFFECTIVELY NO CLOSE SEASON: *see woodpigeon.*

Jays are not territorial and the Larsen trap does not therefore work – though baiting the trap may occasionally prove successful. However, control of jays is generally not that important and some keepers feel their screeching offers an early warning system when all is not well in their coverts.

## Crow – CARRION & HOODED (*CORVUS CORONE CORONE & CORVUS CORONE CORNIX*)

ORIGINALLY THOUGHT TO BE a separate species, the 'hoodie' is now considered to be a subspecies of the carrion crow. Found throughout the British Isles the hooded crow is, generally, restricted to Scotland and Ireland whilst the carrion crow is found in southern Scotland, England and Wales. Where their range overlaps they will freely interbreed.

The two birds are identical in size and shape but the black and pale grey plumage tells the hooded crow from the all black carrion. Both are similar in habits.

Crows become territorial in the spring and keep other crows and magpies away from their nesting site which is usually in a tree, bush, cliff ledge or, sometimes, in the case of the hooded crow on treeless islands, on the ground. Non-territorial birds often form flocks during the summer.

Four or five pale blue or green eggs, speckled and mottled with brown are laid in this large nest of twigs and leaves in about April or May. The young fly at about five weeks and family parties are often seen through to the spring. In winter, the crows may gather in flocks, roosting together, which often leads to the assumption that they are rooks.

As with other corvids, crows are omnivorous and grain, seeds, insects, carrion and eggs feature in their diet. It is debatable whether the crow is less welcome than the magpie from the gamekeeper's point of view but there is no doubt that, of all the corvids, both are the biggest offenders and in Scotland, where the magpie is neither abundant nor widespread, the hoodie is enemy number one. Crows share the magpie's ability to find the nests of other birds and predation of eggs and young can be a serious problem.

65

*Carrion crow*

*Hooded crow*

THERE IS EFFECTIVELY NO CLOSE SEASON: *see woodpigeon.*

As with the magpie, shooting is somewhat impractical. Control is only necessary in the spring and summer and, being aggressively territorial, the Larsen trap has proved to be fairly effective. Crows can even be caught when the decoy bird is a magpie. Cage traps can be effective with the flocking non-territorial birds.

Dogs find all corvids have an unpleasant taste and it is common to encourage them to retrieve these birds. If a dog willingly picks a crow, it is unlikely to refuse a woodcock. However, it is important to be careful when sending a dog to retrieve any corvid lest they be wounded. They can give a savage peck, often aimed at the eyes, and at best can lead a dog to become hard-mouthed.

# Rook *(CORVUS FRUGILEGUS)*

THE ROOK, A MEMBER of the crow family, is a common sight throughout much of the British Isles. Most abundant on mixed arable land they can also be found, quite tame, in towns.

Seen close to, the rook is easily distinguishable from the carrion crow, having a glossier black plumage, squarer shaped head, a bald area of skin on the face at the base of its bill and loose thigh feathers. In flight the rook has a faster wing beat and often the bald patches on the face can be seen. The call is a less harsh 'Kaah' than that of the crow.

In February rooks start re-patching their old nests in the rookeries which can vary from a few pairs to several thousand. Rookeries – some thought to be hundreds of years old – can be found in parkland or woodland and the bulky nests of twigs are usually sited in large trees such as oaks, elms and horse chestnuts. Rooks only defend a territory immediately around their nest and, consequently, a tree may be used by several pairs. The four or five eggs are laid in March or April and young rooks, which lack the bald face, will often be seen on the edge of the nest and surrounding branches in early May before they make their first flight.

Rooks have a varied diet of insects, larvae, worms, grain and carrion. They can create considerable damage to the young shoots of

*Rookery*

crops, although they possess the typical wary corvid nature and a few dead rooks left lying on the field will often put them off. Whilst they will take eggs – and can cause extensive nest losses to gamebirds – they are more opportunistic thieves than active hunters of nests.

Rooks are very sociable birds throughout the year and enormous flocks gather outside the breeding season especially in the evenings when they flight to their roosting woods.

THERE IS EFFECTIVELY NO CLOSE SEASON: *see woodpigeon.*

Due to their wariness, rooks are not easy to shoot. Controlling numbers by shooting is rather ineffective, even at the rookery in the breeding season, and the traditional rook shoots are rarely held now. The gamekeeper and farmer, visited by rooks from a neighbour's rookery, are fighting a losing battle. However, the former will sometimes be successful with a large baited cage trap with a dead sheep (and only needs to worry about them in the spring) and the latter will, generally, get by with pigeon scaring devices.

# *Jackdaw* (CORVUS MONEDULA)

THE JACKDAW IS COMMON and widespread in the British Isles and is often found amongst large flocks of rooks. They are sociable birds and rarely seen singly.

The jackdaw is considerably smaller than the crow and is unlikely to be confused with the hoodie, the grey of its plumage being restricted to the head only. Crows and rooks have much more noticeable primary feather 'fingers' and slower wingbeats than jackdaws. The jackdaw's call, which immediately gives their presence away in large flocks of rooks, is a fairly high pitched 'Kow' and a quieter 'Chack'.

The nest can be sited in the hole of a tree, crack in a cliff or in buildings – often church towers – and frequently several pairs will form small colonies, returning each year. The 4–6 eggs are laid in April or May and the young are cared for by both parents.

The jackdaw's diet is similar to the other corvids and they will take eggs and young of other birds but, like the rook, this is more through opportunity than active hunting.

There is effectively no close season (see woodpigeon) though, as with other corvids,

control is only necessary in the spring. The effect of predation is fairly minor when compared to the crow and magpie and time is probably better spent trying to deal with these two rather than the jackdaw.

## OTHER PEST BIRDS

### *Coot* (*FULICA ATRA*)

FOUND THROUGHOUT MUCH of the British Isles, both as a resident and winter visitor, the coot is a common sight on large ponds in towns and cities and its habits are much the same in the country where it frequents lakes, reservoirs and gentle flowing rivers.

The curious rounded, dumpy shape makes this bird easy to identify. The coot is effectively black all over except for its white bill and forehead shield and grey-green legs. The toes are partially webbed enabling it to both walk and swim fairly well but not masterfully. The call is a sharp 'Kek' varying in pitch.

This strongly aggressive bird begins to defend a territory around its nest site in February and squabbles between pairs are frequent and savage – long scuttling runs across the water ending in pitched battles as the birds rise up out of the water, clawing at each other. The nest is a large construction made of reeds and is anchored to bankside vegetation, sometimes hidden but often clearly visible. The first clutch of about 7–10 eggs is generally laid in late March or early April and incubated by both male and female. The rather ugly chicks can leave the nest shortly after hatching though return to it to be brooded by either parent for a few days. Both parents supply food for the young until quite well grown. The chicks

*Nest*

can often be seen waiting for the adults to bob up ungracefully from the depths. A second brood is common.

Coots are predominantly vegetarian but will supplement this diet with insects and tadpoles etc. as well as eggs and chicks of other birds, though more often than not the attacking of ducklings is a defensive action when they stray too close to their nest or brood.

SEASON:
*Great Britain: September 1 – January 31*
*Northern Ireland: fully protected*

Unless shot frequently, coots are generally rather tame and often hardly bother to swim away from humans, though they usually cannot be

approached when out of the water. Even when relatively wild they will swim in preference to flying, unless pushed. This flight is usually a pattering run across the water surface and coots take a considerable amount of time to get airborne. Once actually off the water the coot has a fairly slow and laboured flight, low to the surface, and often lands a few seconds later, finding security in the reeds.

Coot shooting is, consequently, not about testing targets but a matter of reducing numbers when too many duck nests are being predated and, in the case of wildfowl collections, too much food being taken. Flight ponds are often too small for coots and therefore this latter situation does not normally arise.

The problem, of course, is that thinning the population by way of an annual cull in

January leaves ample time for more coots to take up residence before ducks start to nest and numbers can build up remarkably quickly, thus making the whole procedure rather pointless.

Watch birds that you think have been hit – they rarely seem to flinch but will often be found dead in the reeds where they landed. Wounded coots dive readily and a dog is essential, but be extremely careful of ricochets from water.

## *M*oorhen (GALLINULA CHLOROPUS)

THE MOORHEN, MEREHEN OR waterhen, like the coot, is found almost throughout the British Isles, in both towns and the countryside. Almost any area of water will satisfy the moorhen from reservoirs to small

ponds, streams and even water-filled ditches. They can often be found some distance from water (usually when searching for food) and are frequently seen in meadows and fields, especially on stubbles. The moorhen's diet is much the same as that of the coot and they will rarely ignore an egg, but this is more opportunistic predation rather than deliberate.

Moorhens are easily distinguished from coots by the white stripe along the flank, white flitting under-tail coverts and the red and yellow bill and red forehead shield which is less prominent than the coot's. There are two main calls: a gentle 'Prruk', often heard at night, and a high pitched 'Ittik' repeated in courtship battles and squabbles and often heard in response to a loud noise such as a shot.

The nest is similar to the coot's, anchored to bankside vegetation or branches protruding

from the water but can also be found on land and even low down in bushes. The 6–10 eggs are laid in April and there can be two or three broods in a year. Like the coot, the parent birds feed the young which use the nest as a base for the first few days.

The moorhen's feet are not webbed and it is a slow and laboured swimmer, nodding jerkily like a chicken, but it can run fast on land. Moorhens are quite at home in trees, often roosting in them, and frequently take to bushes when danger threatens.

SEASON:
*Great Britain: September 1 – January 31*
*Northern Ireland: fully protected*

Moorhens are less happy with man's presence and will tend to swim or fly to bankside reeds and cover. However they feel quite safe in bushes from which they are extremely reluctant to flush.

When they do flush, they usually make a short flight to cover though, unlike the coot, they manage to get airborne relatively quickly. It is on pheasant drives that they are presented at their best which is rarely anything but a poor, ungainly and descending flight.

After a 40 mph pheasant they are remarkably slow and frequently missed as a result.

Moorhens can reach excessive and troublesome numbers if left unchecked, eating a considerable amount of food put out for ducks and at high levels damage to duck nests and broods is unavoidable.

*Adult*

# Gulls — GREAT BLACK-BACKED, LESSER BLACK-BACKED & HERRING GULL (*LARUS MARINUS, LARUS FUSCUS & LARUS ARGENTATUS*)

OF THE THREE SPECIES of gull on the British quarry list, the great black-backed is probably the most easily identified due to its large size. A common bird along the coast, though it tends not to breed in eastern England, it is rarely found inland. Adults have a heavier yellow bill than the lesser black-backed and herring gull but share the red spot on the bottom mandible. The back is almost black and the legs are pink.

The British race of the lesser black-backed is similar to the herring gull, though the back is a darker grey, the back of the Scandinavian race, which visits in winter, being darker still. Both sub-species have yellow legs. The lesser black-backed is found most commonly on the coast, though frequently seen inland, and breeds in the west and some local areas on the east coast.

The herring gull is found across the British Isles, generally breeding near the coast on cliff ledges, buildings and moorland bogs etc. The adult has a pale grey back, pink legs and is much the same size as the lesser black-backed gull.

Gulls generally nest in colonies and both parents share incubation and brood-rearing. Immatures of all three are similar, being a mottled brown and white and can take three years to attain adult plumage.

*Lesser black-backed*

The diet consists of fish, eggs and chicks of other birds, seaweed, grain, carrion and refuse. The great black-backed will also take small birds and mammals.

THERE IS EFFECTIVELY NO CLOSE SEASON: *see woodpigeon.*

Gulls only need be shot to protect such things as tern colonies and, perhaps, nesting partridges on coastal shoots. They rarely cause problems elsewhere and should, on the whole, be left alone.

*Starling in winter*

## Starling (STURNUS VULGARIS)

ONE OF OUR MOST abundant and widespread birds, the starling is especially common in towns, cities and around farm buildings where tightly packed, wheeling flocks of several thousand are not uncommon.

The irridescent green and purple summer plumage is closely spotted with white in winter. Starlings have short, pointed wings and a fast, direct flight often broken by periods of gliding. They have a wide vocabulary and can mimic other birds and even the human whistle.

Nests can be found in cliffs, tree holes,

eaves of buildings and drainpipes etc. Two broods between April and July are common. The juvenile plumage is a pale brown.

The large concentrations are found outside the breeding season when the build up of droppings beneath their roosts, both on buildings and in trees, can cause much damage.

THERE IS EFFECTIVELY NO CLOSE SEASON: *see woodpigeon.*

Starlings are often accepted by farmers because of the pest insects they eat. Shooting is rarely effective but their apparent unpleasant taste means that they are sometimes used to encourage young dogs, reluctant to retrieve woodcock and snipe.

## House Sparrow (PASSER DOMESTICUS)

THE HOUSE SPARROW IS closely associated with man throughout the British Isles and is found in gardens, towns, cities and on farms.

The male is similar to the tree sparrow, but has a grey crown and rump and lacks the black spot on its cheeks. The female is brown above with buffish underparts.

Nests are sited in ivy, hedges, trees or buildings and up to about three broods can be reared, usually between April and August. House sparrows will often spend much time amongst ripening cereal crops in late summer and may congregate around grain stores on farms during the winter.

THERE IS EFFECTIVELY NO CLOSE SEASON: *see woodpigeon.*

Shooting, to protect grain stores, would need to be constant to have any effect and the disturbance is likely to have more effect than any reduction in numbers. The risk of damage from using anything larger than a garden gun or air rifle so close to buildings probably outweighs the loss of grain.

# DEER

## Red Deer (CERVUS ELAPHUS)

THE NATIVE RED DEER is our largest wild animal and was originally a woodland species. However, in Scotland, where the natural forest has been removed, they have adapted to life on the open hill. At one time more widespread, they are now restricted to Scotland, the west country and small isolated pockets across the rest of the British Isles.

The red deer has a reddish-brown summer coat, becoming longer and greyish-brown in winter, and mature stags develop a mane around their necks in the autumn. The tail is fairly short and surrounded by a yellowish-buff rump patch.

Antlers consist of a main beam out of which a series of tines – brow, bez and trez – grow. Above these is the crown and a stag with all his 'rights' (tines) and three points on top each side is a Royal. Antler development in all deer is dependent on the quality of their food, requiring a constant supply of protein. Therefore, a red stag that makes Royal (twelve points) on the open hill in Scotland has done well whilst a beast in Devon can achieve the same head at a younger age and is more likely to do so. Antlers reach a peak and then start to 'go back' in old age. A mature stag that grows

two long, curved spears, and no other points above the brow tine is called a switch and is shot on sight to save other stags from horrific injuries in the rut, regardless of whether it may throw a good head in the following year. Occasionally, a stag will develop no antlers. This is a permanent abnormality and the beast is called a hummel or, in south-west England, a nott stag.

In late summer, the stags need to lay down fat reserves to see them through the rut, when they have little time for feeding. The rut starts in late September when the stags can be heard roaring in order to establish dominance and attract hinds, wallowing in peat hags to make themselves look blacker and stronger than other stags. They guard a harem of hinds, rather than a territory, constantly keeping them from straying. Harems can number 20 hinds or more and the stag loses considerable weight in the constant battles with rivals. On the open hill, a stag less than about 5 or 6 years old is unlikely to keep a harem of his own and will wander between groups trying his luck.

The rut finishes towards the end of October and, generally, the stags will form bachelor herds, the hinds remaining in groups of about 8 to 20. The advancing winter brings these hind groups together as they come down for the better feeding and herds of two or three hundred are not uncommon. If the weather is not too bad, they will spend the day up on the tops, more or less at rest, and come down to feed at night. Generally the hinds are found higher up than the stags and come down later for the better

*Calf*

feeding, possibly due to those with calves at foot feeling safer on higher ground. Run stags (those which have held harems) take a considerable amount of time to recover. Many take advantage of the quality feeding on arable land and run the risk of being shot as marauding deer, legally, out of season. In years of heavy rain, some will simply curl up and die as will many yearling beasts, especially knobbers (stags) now without the benefit of their mothers beside them. Stags that have not held harems will usually survive well. The antlers are cast towards the end of April, new growth starting immediately, and are usually clean of velvet – a soft tissue supplying nutrients to the growing antler – in September.

The hinds break up into smaller groups once more at the end of winter and will drop a single dappled calf (very rarely twins) around June, rejoining the group once it is able to keep up. The calf will usually stay with the hind until after she gives birth the following year.

Although they will browse, red deer are mostly grazing animals, feeding on heather and grasses, and, during the summer on the open hill, are active throughout the day amid periods of rest when they chew the cud. In the south – and north in winter – crop damage can be considerable.

SEASONS:

STAGS: *July 1 – October 20 (Scotland)*
*August 1 – April 30 (elsewhere)*
HINDS: *October 21 – February 15 (Scotland)*
*November 1 – February 28 (elsewhere)*

The word 'stalking' more aptly refers to red deer on the open hill where you spy the deer first and then stalk to within a reasonable range. Given the huge acreages that deer forests cover, the stalker must know roughly where the deer will be, whatever the conditions and, having spied a shootable beast, must know the ground intimately, use every

contour and be constantly aware of any changes in the wind, in a land which can appear so remarkably open and devoid of cover that approach seems impossible. Throughout, it is essential to know exactly where the herd is and to be aware of other factors which may influence the direction of the stalk. The sudden disturbance of sheep or loud flush of grouse – which invariably fly straight towards the herd calling 'go back' – can easily alarm the deer and send them away.

On reaching the point of shot, the stalker or ghillie will guide you over the placing of the shot itself. If he suggests exactly where to aim it is well worth taking the advice and may save you both a lot of time in following up a wounded beast. He will also be watching for the reaction to the shot. A neck shot will drop the beast immediately. At longer distances, a broadside shot placed in the front box – behind the shoulder but not as far back as the end of the rib cage – will cover the lungs or, low down, behind the elbow, the heart.

A heart-shot deer will react with an immediate constriction of the body and simultaneous spring and may run off 50 yards or more before slowing, stopping and falling dead. Hit in the lungs, the deer may run immediately, often 50–100 yards or more but sometimes will simply walk round slowly and then go down. A badly misplaced shot in the belly will produce a similar body constriction to the heart shot but not so sharp and there is no spring, the deer moving off slowly 200 yards or so, if it has not seen anyone, and lying down in cover. This latter shot will produce a loud hollow sound of the bullet strike. You will need to re-stalk this beast carefully or you may never recover it.

The general aim should be to take a good age cross section of the stags. Except for the very old, you should try to gauge what sort of head they will show the following year – a small bump on the beam could make another point – and, generally, there is a preference to leave the wider spreading heads. Most stalkers will also shoot a hummel but they can be much larger beasts and some argue that they produce good stags in their offspring – being bigger and stronger they will often successfully hold a harem.

With the hind cull – and the culling of does and hinds of all deer – if you have time to pick and choose you should take the old: those with long, thin, pointed faces with grey around the muzzle; a big belly, suggesting middle-aged spread; a curved back and a poor calf at foot. And on that point, having dropped a hind, if a calf remains behind with its mother – and it is often impossible to tell which have calves – it is considered kind to shoot it as it will not survive on the open hill. Finally, lame or injured animals should automatically be taken.

*Stag in velvet*

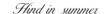

*Hind in summer*

*Stag in winter*

74

*Dappled and
black fallow bucks*

# Fallow Deer (DAMA DAMA)

BELIEVED TO HAVE BEEN introduced into Great Britain by the Normans, the fallow is still a traditional parkland deer but escapees have established themselves in the wild across most of the British Isles.

Smaller than the red deer, the fallow has two main colour variations: the dappled and the black. The former is a rich russet in summer, spotted with white, and has creamy-white underparts. In winter it is darker with less noticeable spots. The black fallow ranges

from mid-brown to almost black with paler underparts and, on closer inspection, an indication of spots. The tail, quite long compared to other deer, is dark above, standing out against the dark edged white rump, and is swished from side to side almost continuously.

The mature buck has large, wide-spreading, palmated antlers with points, or 'spellers', forming a ragged rear edge. Yearling bucks, called prickets, grow two straight spikes and successive heads will show tines on the main beam and a gradual increase in the palmation.

Found in any type of woodland, they have a preference for mature, lowland, deciduous woods. It has also been suggested that fallow favour heavy land and, indeed, the larger concentrations are often found on the heaviest ground. Fallow browse and graze equally and, in woods where there are large numbers, a browsing line can often be seen with little or no cover from the ground up to the limit of their reach. Except in the rut, they can frequently be found

*Doe, pricket and fawn*

lying out away from cover during the day, in areas of little disturbance. However, they generally become active towards dusk and tend to emerge from wooded cover later than other deer and the older beasts seem to become more nocturnal.

Antlers are cast in April or May and the new set is clean of velvet at the end of August. The rut is usually in late October or early November and the traditional rutting stands, used for many generations, are commonly found in small wooded

clearings. The dominant, or master buck, will take control of the stand and defend it from other bucks, as opposed to defending the does. The does are usually to be found nearby within the wood and, as they come into season, will visit their chosen master buck for mating. A wood of 20–30 acres might have 2 or 3 master bucks which seem to tolerate each other, recognising the separate stands, but will immediately charge any lesser bucks and prickets. The rut lasts two or three weeks, at the end of which the big bucks seem to vanish and a typical herd will consist of 20 does and their

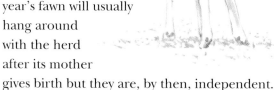

fawns, 5 or 6 prickets and possibly the odd small antlered buck.

The does drop single, spotted fawns in June. The previous year's fawn will usually hang around with the herd after its mother gives birth but they are, by then, independent.

Fallow deer are wanderers and can move over considerable areas during the night and, therefore, to manage a herd properly, the stalker needs to have the shooting over a large area of land.

SEASONS:
BUCKS: *August 1 – April 30*
DOES: *October 21 – February 15 (Scotland)*
*November 1 – February 28 (elsewhere)*

Considered by some to be the wariest and hardest to stalk, fallow deer can certainly look after themselves. Several animals may be taken from a herd of red deer but with fallow, generally, one shot will send them running.

There are several methods of shooting woodland deer. Woodland stalking, often called 'still hunting', is less about stalking than creeping, very quietly, in and along the edges of woods, hoping that a chance will present itself. The stalker is usually unaware of any deer until the last moment but will sometimes need to actually stalk a beast to reach a safe point of shot or one that offers a clear shot. The term 'stalking' is more appropriate when the deer are found out in the open, either feeding or resting, and ditches, hedges, shelter belts etc. will usually provide an approach of sorts.

Many woodland deer are shot from high seats or from cover overlooking an area where they are expected to appear – woodland rides and clearings or quiet well used fields. Generally, high seats are more effective in the evenings and one should get quietly into position well before dusk. Walking out to a high seat before dawn could easily disturb the deer which emerged from cover the evening before. However, it is important to stop before it gets too dark. You may be able to pick up a deer in the 'scope and place a reasonably accurate shot but, in the event of one that runs, you will need to mark the spot where it enters cover. High seats offer two distinct advantages over shooting from the ground: you are less likely to be seen, as deer rarely look for danger from above, and the shot will be angled more towards the ground and is, therefore, safer.

The other main method of shooting woodland deer is by 'moving'. More about controlling excessive numbers, this can often work well with just one beater walking quietly and steadily through a small wood and, certainly, the less people involved the safer it will be. The direction the deer take on being disturbed will be learned by trial and error and the rifle should be concealed, overlooking a safe shooting area. Emerging from cover, disturbed deer will often stop two or three times, before reaching the next wood, and look back to see what all the fuss was about.

With all methods of deer stalking, when a shot is taken always pause for a few minutes. If the deer is missed and has not seen you it will often run a short distance and then stop, perhaps offering another chance. A wounded deer will head for the nearest cover and find a place to lie down but if it sees you it will keep going. Many stalkers will take a specifically trained dog to follow up wounded deer.

## Roe Deer (CAPREOLUS CAPREOLUS)

WIDESPREAD AND COMMON IN the north and south, the roe, like the red, is a native to Great Britain. Smaller than the fallow, the roe stands a little over 2ft at the shoulder. It is a beautiful and elegant animal with a triangular facial profile, a black nose and a white chin. Between about April and October the coat is a bright reddish-brown with an indistinct rump patch, changing to grey-brown with a cream or white rump in its longer winter coat. The tail is not visible but the rump flares with erectile hairs when alarmed and both the buck and doe will often bark sharply and repeatedly as they run off. A mature buck's antlers may only be 8 or 10 inches long and usually consist of three tines on each, the lower one pointing forward, the next backwards and the third upright. The pearling on the main beam increases towards the base where the coronets seem to fuse together. Bucks cast their antlers in November and the new set are clean of velvet in mid to late April. The

*Roe doe*

*Buck*

'perruque' head is a grossly deformed antler of velvet covered, spongy, tissue caused by injury to the testes and is never cast.

Roe are predominantly found in younger and thicker woodland than fallow and, even in Scotland where they venture out onto the open moorland, are seldom found very far from the forest or plantations.

Roe deer territories, which are marked with scent glands, can cover quite large areas depending on the density of the population. The rut is at the end of July and beginning of August and they are thought, possibly, to be polygamous although the buck does not gather a harem and will often associate with a single doe.

Kids are born in June and the seemingly long gestation is explained by a delayed implantation of the embryo. Twins are more common than single kids and triplets often occur. Predation of kids by foxes is not a major problem. The buck kid shows his first head of two little buttons on pedicles at about 6 months and these are shed at 8 months when the first real antlers begin to grow. Generally the family, with or without the buck, will stay together as a group through to the following summer.

Roe are less nocturnal than fallow deer and can often be seen feeding during the day. They browse more than they graze and can cause a lot of damage in young plantations both by feeding and fraying the bark on young trees – to remove velvet and also as a territorial mark. Scrapes, made by pawing the ground around trees, are further territorial

signs but they will also make scrapes in which to lie during the day.

SEASONS:
BUCKS: *April 1 – October 31 (England & Wales)*
*April 1 – October 20 (Scotland)*
DOES: *November 1 – February 28 (England & Wales)*
*October 21 – March 31 (Scotland)*

*In velvet*

78

When roebuck stalking, the aim is, once again, to take a range of ages. Take the old buck with blunted points – noticeable belly, head held low and a thick neck (though the neck of an even older buck will get thinner); leave the middle-aged buck (thick neck but raised head) with a nice uniform head and take the grotesquely large and the small; leave the young buck with a good evenly-shaped head. And, finally, take those with little or no pearling.

Waiting up, in a high seat at dusk, in late spring, for a roebuck to emerge can be one of the most idyllic and peaceful forms of shooting – the calming of birds and animals after the frantic bustle of a spring day; a duck, cackling in anger, pursued by two or three drakes, pinions whistling overhead in their acrobatic chase; a fox pouncing on a mouse under a clump of grass and the croaking of a roding woodcock, flickering past so close you can almost touch it.

*Sika stag*

*Summer*

*Winter*

## $S$*ika Deer* (CERVUS NIPPON)

THREE SUB-SPECIES OF SIKA (Formosan, Manchurian and Japanese) were introduced into deer parks in the British Isles in the 1800s. Escapees have led to isolated populations in the wild – mostly of the smaller Japanese sika, although the sub-species will interbreed and even hybridize with red deer.

The summer coat, generally, resembles that of the dappled fallow deer – though the Japanese sika is a little smaller. The antlers are vaguely similar to those of a young red stag, consisting of a main beam and usually four points on each side with mature beasts. The biggest heads, occasionally 10 or 12 points in total, are found in south-west England. In winter they grow a longer dark brown coat without spots but the dark edged white rump is noticeable at all times of the year.

Antlers are cast between late March and mid-May and the new set are clean of velvet around September. The rut runs from late September to late October. Sika are sometimes found in mixed herds in winter but otherwise, except during the rut, in small single sex

*Roe kid*

*Sika hind*

groups and are active mostly between dusk and dawn, both browsing and grazing. Predominantly a woodland and heathland deer, they can occasionally, in good weather, be found up on the tops of the open hill.

Hinds drop single calves in June or July. Stag calves will leave their mothers at about 9 months, joining a bachelor group, whilst hind calves will remain until about a year old.

SEASONS:

STAGS: *July 1 – October 20 (Scotland)*
       *August 1 – April 30 (elsewhere)*
HINDS: *October 21 – February 15*
       *(Scotland)*
       *November 1 – February 28*
       *(elsewhere)*

# Reeves Muntjac (MUNTIACUS REEVESI)

THE LITTLE MUNTJAC WAS introduced into deer collections about 100 years ago and escapees successfully established themselves in the wild. Their range is steadily increasing in southern England.

Only likely to be confused with the similar sized Chinese water deer, the coat of the muntjac is a rich rufous, changing to a greyer brown in winter. Two dark stripes run up the forehead, meeting on the crown of the doe and continuing up the long and prominent pedicles of the buck. Muntjac have deep facial scent glands, between and in the corners of their eyes.

Mature bucks carry antlers consisting of two short curved spikes, sometimes with a small tine close to the base, and display long canine teeth as tusks. Muntjac have a plump, somewhat hunch-backed appearance, holding their heads low, and when disturbed, run off with their tails held up high. Bucks have a loud

*Muntjac buck*

*Muntjac*

80

bark which may be repeated for up to an hour during the rut or when alarmed.

Whilst the antlers are cast annually, muntjac, which are territorial, have a 7 month breeding cycle and fawns, usually singles, can therefore be born at any time of year. Fawns lose their spots at about 8 weeks old.

Muntjac are fairly solitary, or found in pairs, and favour woodland with thick brambly ground cover though they will also use tall arable crops. They are generally active between dusk and dawn but will feed during the day if relatively undisturbed. Whilst they are predominantly browsers, they also feed on forest mast and fruit.

As muntjac do not have a fixed breeding period, there is no close season. If a doe appears to be pregnant then it is reasonable to assume that she does not have a dependent fawn. That leaves you with the problem of the ethics of shooting a pregnant animal. Take care when using dogs to follow up a wounded buck – the long canines make fearsome weapons.

## Chinese Water Deer
### (HYDROPOTES INERMIS)

INTRODUCED INTO DEER PARKS in the early 1900s, some Chinese water deer, as with other non-native species, escaped into the surrounding countryside in south-eastern England where they have adapted well enough to be included on the British quarry list.

Much the same size as the muntjac, Chinese water deer do not have the characteristic hunched appearance and bucks do not grow antlers. Instead the buck shows very long canine tusks – more noticeable than those of the muntjac – and the doe smaller ones. The tail is very short and the bright yellowish-brown summer coat turns a duller grey-brown in winter.

Water deer are found in thickish woodland with nearby grassland on which they generally feed. They are territorial and often encountered singly or in pairs excepting does with several young. The rut extends through much of the winter and the doe will give birth to her fawns in May or June. Twins are probably most common but 3 or 4 frequently occur and more have been known.

Like the muntjac, chinese water deer have no close season, though, as they have a fixed breeding period, the reason for this is not certain. At present, there is little need for control.

## RABBITS AND HARES

## Rabbit (ORYCTOLAGUS CUNICULUS)

INTRODUCED INTO BRITAIN BY the Normans, the rabbit's success story nearly ended with the appearance of myxomatosis in the 1950's, which resulted in an immediate and drastic decline.

The rabbit can recover from the disease but, such is the effect upon its senses, it generally falls prey to predators and cannot find food easily. Those that do recover pass on a certain ammount of immunity to their young and in recent years the rabbit has increased dramatically, though the disease will usually resurface to keep numbers in check when densities are high.

A blend of colours produce a brown coat with a white belly although there are variations, presumably due to tame rabbit escapees. Bucks and does are not easy to tell apart although the doe's head is narrower. The doe is also smaller but at any time of year there can be rabbits of varying age and size and this is consequently never a reliable indicator of sex.

Whilst, at long distances, the rabbit can sometimes be confused with the hare, the general shape and posture usually tells the two apart. The rabbit is much smaller and the ears shorter and not tipped with black. When running, its short white tail is held up and clearly visible whilst the hare's is held down, showing the dark upper surface. The rabbit scurries, the hare lollops.

Whilst rabbits are often found above ground during the day, and some live above ground, the majority feed at night on a diet consisting of grass, weeds and most things that the farmer or gardener grows. Tree damage usually occurs in winter and if there is little food about they can ring the bark of well grown trees and cause extensive losses in plantations.

Their burrows can be found both in the open and amongst thick cover. Warren sizes vary enormously, with some consisting of only 2 or 3 holes whilst an attractive bank can be peppered with dozens. Rabbits will also frequently make little scrapes out in the middle of a field.

Whilst rabbits can be born at any time of year, the main breeding period is between January and June. The young are born blind, deaf and naked and are cared for by the doe. After only a month, they are independent and the doe is quite capable of having another litter but, whilst rabbits have become famous for their breeding habits the mortality rate is high. Foxes, stoats, weasels and buzzards are amongst their many predators. Such is the terror instilled in the rabbit by the stoat, they find that they are unable to increase their speed and, after a monotonous and rather gentle chase, the rabbit gives up.

Rabbits have no close season but, as most are shot at night under a lamp, the height of the crops by late spring allows them some protection and the most intensive shooting is therefore usually after harvest. Great care must be taken when handling guns in vehicles, especially at night and over bumpy fields. Whilst the safety catch is rather more certain on a rifle than a shotgun, .22 rounds are prone to ricochets. Safe shots often being impossible with a rifle, it is probably better to stick to a shotgun.

The most testing way to shoot rabbits is either with ferrets or while rough shooting with a dog, offering tantalising glimpses as they bolt for another patch of cover. In the latter case, either extreme care or a very steady dog is required.

A solo expedition, creeping round the hedgerows with a rifle or shotgun will test fieldcraft rather than shooting skill, but is more a method of obtaining one for the pot than an effective way of controlling rabbits. The unskilled will generally hear the rabbit's warning thump but see little.

Rabbits can do a considerable amount of damage and where they are present in reasonable numbers, only constant shooting pressure will keep them in check. Half-hearted forays are not an effective control.

## *B*rown Hare (*Lepus europaeus*)

THE BROWN HARE is a native to Great Britain (though not Ireland) and found throughout lowland regions. Declining for many years, they now appear to be holding their own and in some areas increasing, especially where mixed arable land prevails.

*Brown hare*

The hare is a fairly solitary animal, generally seen on its own in the middle of a field which usually distinguishes it from the rabbit. It is considerably larger than the rabbit and has a bony face with prominent eyes and long black-tipped ears. The sexes are alike, although the male is slightly smaller, and the tawny-brown coat offers excellent camouflage, especially in its form where the hare rests during the day. The form is a shallow depression in the ground often out in the middle of a field far from cover. Lying flat and motionless, little of the hare can be seen and their eruption from the ground a few yards in front can be quite startling. Indeed they can sit so tight that it is sometimes possible to walk straight past them within a foot or two and even quite well grown leverets can occasionally be picked up by hand.

Courtship explains the antics of the mad March hare, though such sights are often encountered in February. Standing up on their hind legs and boxing, the doe repels the buck's advances and, together with their graceful flowing and leaping chases, provides a fascinating display and a promise of spring.

The doe can have three or four litters of 2–4 leverets a year. The leverets, not having the protection of a burrow, are born furred and with their eyes open and are often left by the doe in different forms, presumably to reduce the predation risk to the whole litter. When

*Boxing*

disturbed, the doe will leave her young, often lolloping slowly away towards a favoured crossing point in a hedge, doubling back on the far side and returning to the leverets by a round-about route.

During the winter, hares will often move into the warmth of thick hedges and woodland. They browse and graze and can cause considerable damage in plantations but, generally, unless in great numbers, hares do little harm to the farmer.

SEASON:
*there is no close season but hares may not be killed on Sundays or Christmas day. However, there is technically a season on moorland and unenclosed non-arable land. Rather typically the law is both confusing and ambiguous. The B.A.S.C. at Marford Mill, Rossett, Wrexham, Clwyd would be happy to explain and advise. It is illegal to sell or offer hares for sale between March 1 and July 31 inclusive.*

The traditional hare shoot in February is now not as common as it once was. As numbers increase so does damage and generally this will be dealt with by an organised shoot every few years which can seriously reduce the population. On these occasions 40 or more guns may turn out, split

into two teams, half walking, half standing. The drives are long, bringing in many fields, and the shooting often dangerous, with instructions frequently ignored. But taking part in such a day on a well keepered shoot will provide one with some beautiful sights, not only of hares but also of other game as the line passes through spinneys and shelter belts.

At other times, hares are shot on driven pheasant days – where ground game is allowed – or when rough shooting as occasional extras, especially from sugar beet and stubbles. Many will be seen on partridge drives but are usually ignored.

Hares are beautiful animals and deserve more than they get by way of seasonal protection. However, most land owners care enough to control them sensibly and many guns turn a blind eye when a hare crosses through a fence at a favoured spot, raising their caps instead of their barrels. If you choose to shoot them only take them at close range and always watch them until they are out of sight as it can take a lot to kill them cleanly.

# *B*lue Hare *(LEPUS TIMIDUS SCOTICUS)*

THE BLUE, OR SCOTTISH mountain, hare is, as the latter name implies, found on mountainous moorland.

Somewhat smaller than the brown hare, the blue has shorter ears and its tail, lacking the dark upper parts, is wholly white. The summer coat of dusky greyish or reddish-brown generally turns completely white in winter except for the tips of the ears which remain black throughout the year. However, there are exceptions and the colour change is not necessarily universal. The blue hare gets its name during the moult when the mixture of summer and winter fur blends to give a blue or greyish-brown appearance.

In habits the blue hare is very similar to the brown although it is more likely to take refuge in cover, whether rocky outcrop or thick

*Blue hare during the moult*

85

heather. Predation is mostly by foxes, stoats, buzzards and eagles.

The same seasons and laws regarding the brown hare apply to the blue. As a rule, most blue hares are shot from November to January, once the grouse and stags are finished. Some are taken when walking up grouse but the majority are driven. Whilst the grouse flies along the contours, blue hares generally run uphill when flushed so the guns are usually placed along the top, the beaters tending to walk across and diagonally up towards them.

The Irish hare (*Lepus timidus hibernicus*) is somewhat larger than the blue hare (though smaller than the brown) and is similar in habits. It has red-brown fur in summer and a less complete, more patchy white winter coat.

SEASON:
*Northern Ireland: August 12 – January 31*

*Cub*

## PEST ANIMALS

### *F*ox (*VULPES VULPES*)

THE FOX, A NATIVE to Britain, receives a mixed reaction in the field – from virtual hatred to deep respect. That it has survived must surely provoke, if grudgingly, admiration in anyone. For this survival it must partly thank the hunting world which has cared for it as a keeper cares for his pheasants. But mostly its own ability to adapt has ensured that the fox will be with us for a while yet. And a sad day it would be if this beautiful animal could no longer be seen in the wild.

Initial sightings in towns were met with disbelief but now to see a fox in London is not so remarkable and many people leave food out for them to save their dustbins from a ransacking. Whether this novelty of such a link with the countryside will wear off in time is uncertain but probably unlikely unless rabies hits these shores. However, the fox has already adapted to town life and survives, with or without these titbits, and such 'fox farms' provide a constant stream out into the surrounding countryside to give the keepers an unending headache.

The fox has a rich rufous coat with, effectively, white underparts, extending under the chin and to the cheeks and muzzle. The backs of the ears and the fronts of the legs are black. A thin muzzle, almost permanently pricked ears – giving a very alert expression – and a long, bushy tail tipped with white, make this a superbly elegant animal, emphasised by its light-footed movement. Foxes in Scotland are often much greyer in colour.

86

Foxes are at their most vocal in mid-winter – the eerie screams answering each other as they search for a mate – and fights between dogs are common. Up to half a dozen blind cubs are born around March or April and, after a few weeks, they are weaned off their mother's milk and both the dog and vixen hunt to provide food. The cubbing earth and surrounding area is unmistakable. Areas of vegetation flattened by increasingly aggressive play-fights and countless remains of fur, feather and bone – now the cubs' toys – are a sure sign of their presence and a warm, sunny evening will usually offer the chance to watch their delightful antics. It is, perhaps, unfortunate that partridges, pheasants and other ground nesting birds choose to nest at this time of year. The cubs require ever increasing amounts of food and most wild game losses therefore occur in the spring and early summer.

The vixen will have other earths to which she will carry her young if she senses danger. As they become increasingly adventurous the vixen will begin to take the cubs hunting with her. Then they learn the tricks of her cunning trade, pouncing on beetles and worms and progressing, with initial ineffectiveness, to mice. When the vixen makes a more substantial kill for her cubs the skeleton, minus the head – the fox's trademark – is picked clean, except for the wing feathers, and left behind in their wake.

By late summer the cubs are beginning to hunt on their own. Harvest is a time of plenty and gives the cubs a chance to sharpen their skills for the bleak winter ahead. Foxes are often active well before dark and visiting a release pen before continuing with their often regular routine frequently pays off. Given the chance they will kill as many birds as they can, taking only one to eat and, perhaps, burying a second for another meal – usually in a shallow scrape, with the legs or primary feathers protruding, and often forgotten. Foxes are often heard barking at harvest time and, when meeting others, vicious fights break out as the dogs try to establish a territory.

The fox's diet consists of beetles, voles, mice, rats, rabbits, hares, game and other birds as well as carrion and occasionally lambs. Rabbits, where plentiful, play a major part in the diet but predation to gamebirds is significant. A fox on a well-managed shoot with plenty of wild birds will do most damage in the spring. On a shoot almost entirely dependent on reared birds the problem will be for a month or two after the birds start to leave the release pen.

There is no close season for shooting, though the height of the crops usually gives them one. Without going into the hunting argument the most efficient way to deal with foxes is with a high velocity rifle. No matter what one feels about the habits of the fox, this beautiful animal deserves to be brought down quickly and cleanly. Rim-fire .22's no doubt account for many but, sadly, wound a great

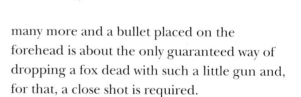

many more and a bullet placed on the forehead is about the only guaranteed way of dropping a fox dead with such a little gun and, for that, a close shot is required.

Arguably the most efficient rifle for foxes is the .22/250 with its very flat trajectory, making it particularly accurate. The bullet fragments on impact delivering tremendous trauma which will be enough, in the event of a badly placed shot, to so disorientate the fox that there is ample time for a second shot. Aiming just behind the elbow or shoulder will offer a large enough target in the front box at 100 yards to allow plenty of room for a pulled shot and at 200–300 yards the fox will drop just as quickly. Indeed this rifle will knock down a fox so fast that the recoil, which is relatively small, will usually leave you wondering whether you hit or missed, though the bullet strike can usually be heard.

*Cub*

Being mostly nocturnal, lamping is the most effective way to shoot foxes with a rifle. At harvest time, young foxes will usually be fascinated by a lamp. Squeaking up a fox involves the rough imitation of a squealing rabbit and will often bring a young fox running from several hundred yards, sometimes resulting in a 15 yard shot. Adult foxes can take a lot of persuading and often shy away from the lamp or move off on hearing the squeak. However, usually the sound will stop them, if only briefly, allowing a shot to be taken. Lamping is not an easy task on one's own unless taking close shots. At 150 yards the fox needs to be right in the centre of the beam to pick it up clearly in the 'scope – not an easy feat when holding both lamp and rifle.

Sitting up in a quiet, likely spot at dusk can be a relatively productive way to shoot foxes especially from mid-summer to mid-autumn when activity during the hour before dark is much more predictable. Often this will be a solitary vigil and consequently you may not be able to tell whether a shot was successful – especially in the fading light. Do not rush out immediately. Wait five minutes or so. A missed fox will frequently poke its head out of cover again.

On other occasions foxes will be shot as incidentals on shooting days. Always ask first whether foxes should be shot if you do not know the form – your host may be a keen hunting man. On driven days there will be few safe chances but it is important to remember that you are using game shot. Only take close shots and aim very much up the front end.

It is considered wise to leave the territorial dog fox which will keep out any intruders. Which leaves you with the problem of deciding which is the resident dog.

## $S$toat (MUSTELA ERMINEA)

THE STOAT, A RELATIVE of the badger, is found throughout Great Britain and a smaller sub-species is found in Ireland.

The stoat has a reddish-brown summer coat with cream or white underparts. The tail is tipped with black and this, together with its much larger size, distinguishes it from the weasel. In Scotland the stoat turns white in winter, retaining its black-tipped tail. The further south one goes the less complete the white winter coat becomes and in the south of England it is quite uncommon to find one of pure white.

The stoat's den is usually in an old burrow or tree stump and there the female produces one litter of up to half a dozen young.

Stoats have poor eyesight and even when pursuing their prey rely considerably on scent. This probably explains the relentless and almost leisurely pace with which they pursue rabbits. The rabbit is so terrified that it seems unable to use its superior speed to outrun its enemy and eventually gives up, screaming in fear.

There is no close season but the chance to shoot a stoat will be rare. Trapping is the only effective control. However, whilst the stoat will take ground nesting birds, it does a certain amount of good in controlling rats and rabbits.

*Weasel*

## Weasel (MUSTELA NIVALIS)

CLOSELY RELATED TO THE STOAT, the weasel is found throughout Great Britain but not in Ireland. It resembles the stoat in both appearance and habits but it is considerably smaller, has a shorter tail which is not tipped with black and has a slightly redder coat which does not turn white in winter. Though it will attack prey much larger than itself, its diet generally consists of small mammals such as rats and mice and, as such, does a lot more good than harm.

There is no close season but it is probably best to leave the weasel alone.

## Mink (LUTREOLA VISON)

MINK WERE ORIGINALLY BROUGHT to Britain for their fur and escapees, somewhat predictably, resulted. 'Wild' mink were first seen back in the 1950s and established themselves in many areas, thanks to an adaptable diet and few major predators.

The problem has been exacerbated by the deliberate release of many thousands of animals from mink farms by those, perhaps understandably, outraged by this form of fur trade. But whilst they congratulate themselves on rescuing animals bred purely for human vanity, they have caused the destruction of far more wildlife than they have saved.

Mink, in Britain, vary in colour from white to dark brown or black. Larger than the stoat, they are ferocious predators. Disasterous to all ground nesting birds, the mink also swims well and fish as well as ducks are regularly taken.

There is no close season but trapping with baited cage traps is the only effective way to deal with mink.

# Grey Squirrel (SCIURUS CAROLINENSIS)

RELEASED FROM ZOOS about a hundred years ago, the grey squirrel rapidly took to the English countryside and is now found almost everywhere in England and Wales and parts of Scotland. The grey squirrel came from America and 'pays us back for the starling' which we gave them. Whilst in America it is a major game species, it is considered a pest in Britain.

Effectively grey with white underparts, there can often be a considerable amount of red, which is more obvious in the shorter summer coat, but there should be no confusion with the red squirrel.

Superbly agile amongst the branches they can leap very large gaps between trees. The drey is built from twigs and leaves, often close to the main trunk and partly hidden by ivy and is therefore not always conspicuous.

Though the squirrel will take eggs and chicks occasionally, its diet is mostly vegetarian – nuts, fruit, berries, buds, seeds and bark. It can cause considerable damage to trees, by bark stripping, and to bird feeders of every kind.

There is no close season and both shotguns and .22s each have their advantages and can, together with trapping, form an effective method of control.

# Rat (RATTUS NORVEGICUS)

THE BROWN RAT CAME to Britain from Asia as a stowaway. Its adaptability has ensured that wherever man can be found it will not be far away, as we provide much of their food and often house them in our outbuildings.

The rat breeds prolifically and its many enemies – fox, weasel, owl and man amongst them – seem to have little impact on their numbers. Food is always at hand whether they have to kill it, steal it or scavenge it. Often found near water, needing to drink, it swims well and is frequently mistaken for the water vole.

The risks of living on a well run shoot, due to the keeper's trapping line, are outweighed by the benefits of food supplied, be it at the flight pond, feed ride or hopper.

Shooting is not an effective control.

# European
## Quarry Species

FOR MANY GUNS IN BRITAIN, the list of quarry species on our own doorstep is diverse enough for the shooting never to become monotonous. But there are some who like to look further afield.

The majority of the British quarry species are to be found across the rest of Europe – indeed, to the shooting man or woman, Spain is synonymous with the wild red-legged partridge – but there is much else besides and I hope the following offers a taste of the variety and a little insight into the habits of some of the more important game birds and animals. It is clearly not possible, within the limited space available, to include more than a handful of each. Perhaps most noticeably missing are the thrushes, which are legal quarry in half a dozen or more European countries and are thought to constitute the largest annual bag of any gamebird. We, in Britain, are quick to criticize but we, too, shoot and eat migratory birds. Indeed, the population is probably able to withstand the shooting pressure as well as the duck population can.

I have given only an indication of the seasons as they inevitably vary from country to country like many aspects of shooting law. The gun, interested in travelling abroad to shoot, should obviously check these first.

*Willow grouse in summer*

# Scandinavian Willow Grouse
## (*Lagopus lagopus lagopus*)

THE NUMEROUS SUB-SPECIES of willow grouse, or willow ptarmigan, which include the red grouse of the British Isles, can be found in Canada, Alaska, Siberia, Mongolia, Russia and Scandinavia. The Scandinavian sub-species ranges across Norway, Sweden, Finland and northern Russia.

In summer, willow grouse possess a rich rufous plumage, similar to that of the red grouse, though the wings remain white. The underparts become increasingly white during the autumn and the winter plumage is completely white except for the dark tail feathers. The feathered legs and feet also remain white throughout the year. Aside from their differing habitat, the combination of a heavier bill and missing dark eyestripe will distinguish the willow grouse from the rock ptarmigan in winter.

During winter, willow grouse are found in willow and birch scrub thickets along streams, rivers and bogs, their diet consisting almost entirely of the twigs, buds and catkins of willow and birch, when snow cover prevents ground foraging. Moving up to more open, low alpine moorland in the spring, willow grouse eat a wider variety of leaves, shoots and seeds of small berry-bearing shrubs. The distance between their summer and winter range is seldom very far, although in northern Russia and Siberia there may be movements of over 100 miles, especially in hard winters.

Establishing a territory in the spring, the cock's plumage is at its most striking. The bright red wattles above the eyes become very conspicuous and the reddish-brown summer plumage covers the head and neck, sprinkling the back and contrasting strongly with the white of the wings and underparts, especially during its predominantly aerial display. Willow grouse are generally monogamous, although cocks may sometimes make bigamous pairings.

The nest is often sited along forest edges amongst low shrubby cover and 6–12 eggs are laid in May or June, the hen re-laying if the nest is predated during the early stages of incubation. The cock guards the incubating hen and helps to rear the chicks which can fly

*Winter*

short distances at about 10 days. Insects are crucial for the first 2 weeks and losses can be high during cold, wet weather. Goshawks are important predators of the chicks whilst nest predation is mostly by corvids, foxes and stoats.

Little management is carried out for the willow grouse, though some moorland burning and tree felling, to encourage regeneration, is practised locally. It is a far cry from the intensive management in the British Isles and, consequently, whilst the overall population is high, density is generally considerably lower than the red grouse.

Willow grouse are shot in the autumn and early winter and, whilst they may be found above the tree line early on, as the season progresses they move down to the more sheltered thickets. Driven shooting is not practical and therefore willow grouse are generally walked up, both on open ground and amongst willow and birch scrub and occasionally they are stalked by hunters on skis.

Pointing dogs are an integral part of the traditional game-shooting scene in continental Europe. There are few breeds more satisfying to watch and it is, perhaps, a cause of some sadness that they find so little favour amongst British roughshooters other than on grouse moors.

*Autumn*

*Cock hazelhen displaying*

# *H*azel Grouse (BONASA BONASIA)

THE HAZEL GROUSE, or hazelhen, ranges from eastern parts of France eastwards to Siberia, extending from Scandinavia in the north to northern Italy and former Yugoslavia in the south. Whilst towards the east the population is thought to be healthy, the range has constricted from the west and there is considerable concern in Europe over their continued decline, with the largest numbers now found in Finland and Sweden.

The hazel grouse is about the size of a red-legged partridge and, as such, is unlikely to be confused with any other woodland gamebird. The sexes are fairly similar with reddish to greyish-brown mottled upper parts, a small crest and a dark sub-terminal band on the tail, broken at the centre. The white underparts are considerably flecked and barred with dark brown and the legs are partly feathered. Cocks have white-bordered black throats and small red combs above the eyes, barely noticeable in the hen whose throat is whitish.

Hazel grouse tend to avoid purely coniferous woodland, generally preferring large areas of mixed forest with a varied understorey and clearings to promote both regeneration and a patchwork of different ages. When snow covers the ground, hazel grouse feed exclusively in trees, mostly eating the buds and catkins of birch and alder, and form snow holes at night for warmth. In hard winters they may only emerge from these burrows to feed for a few hours each day. During the rest of the year, they roost in trees and ground foraging becomes more important – the diet consisting of the shoots, leaves, berries and seeds of shrubs and other vegetation.

The decline of the hazel grouse is thought to be due to habitat loss – the felling and replanting of the natural forest with coniferous plantations. Little or no habitat management is carried out at present, though the concern over losing this beautiful bird will, hopefully, produce more sympathetic forestry practices before it is too late.

There is very little seasonal movement and hazel grouse occupy a fairly small home range throughout the year. Territorial behaviour occurs in the autumn when the pair bonds are thought to be formed and the territory is re-established in the spring – the cock displaying from a tree stump, or other prominent position, fanning his tail and producing a high-pitched squeaking whistle.

The nest is usually sited beneath a tree, or shrub, or amongst tree roots, and 6–11 eggs are laid in April or May. Whilst the pair may remain together for much of the year, incubation and brood-rearing duties are generally carried out by the hen. The chicks, dependent upon insects for the first 1–2 weeks can make very short flights within a week and are able to fly strongly at a month. The broods break up at about 3 months and the birds become fairly solitary or form pairs which may or may not hold together through the winter. Goshawks and pine martens are the most important predators of adult hazel grouse, together with owls, foxes and weasels, whilst nest predation is by corvids, wild boar and squirrels etc. The annual mortality is thought to be about 65–70%.

*Hen*

*Cock*

Shooting seasons fall between August and November when hazel grouse are either walked up or called. They do not hold particularly well to pointing dogs and frequently, when flushed, will burst up with drumming wings and pitch in a tree. Whistling involves the imitation of the cock's territorial song. Practised in the autumn, when the territories are initially established, whistling generally attracts other cocks within range of the hidden hunter.

# *Rock Partridge* (ALECTORIS GRAECA)

THE ROCK, OR GREEK, partridge is effectively the link between the red-legged partridge in the west and the chukar in the east and is found in the European Alps, Italy, Sicily and eastwards through to Greece and Bulgaria. The population is in decline, mainly due to loss and degradation of suitable habitat;

overhunting may, in certain cases, be a contributory factor.

With a very small range overlap in north-western Italy, geographical location usually separates rock and red-legged partridges and the lack of black speckling on the chest will identify the former. To the extreme east, however, there is a similar overlap with the chukar where confusion can easily arise and the two have been known to hybridize. On close inspection, the rock partridge has a whiter throat, finer barring on the flanks, a cleaner black gorget and the black eyestripe is more extensive both above the eye and at the bill. The sexes are almost identical, though hens usually lack spurs, and the call is similar to the red-legged partridge.

Rock partridges inhabit dry and rocky mountainous areas – usually at 2500–4500ft. Their habitat ranges from heathland, pasture and brushy areas to rocky hillsides almost devoid of vegetation and there is usually some movement to lower, more sheltered ground in

winter. A variety of leaves, shoots, seeds and berries are eaten throughout the year together with insects, especially by young chicks and the hens in spring.

The winter coveys begin to break up in February or March as the territories are established and the, generally monogamous, pair bonds formed. The nest is a scrape in the ground, amongst rocks or moderate vegetation, and a clutch of 8–14 eggs is laid in May–June, with renesting occurring in the event of predation. Incubation and brood-rearing is carried out by the hen, although there have been instances of double-clutches, the hen turning one over to the cock. However, generally cocks play no part in parental duties and form single-sex coveys once the eggs have hatched. The chicks make short flights by 10 days and adult plumage is attained at about 9–10 weeks, though they are not fully grown until 3–4 months. During the autumn, family groups tend to mix and merge, forming larger winter coveys of up to 50 birds.

*Shooting seasons fall between September and the end of December.*

Often found in steep and rocky terrain, rock partridge shooting is hard work. They do not hold particularly well to pointers but, due to their habitat and low density population, they can only be hunted effectively by walking up. Tending to run when alarmed, before reluctantly flushing, the gun must either surprise the covey suddenly or expect to take fairly long shots. Once flushed, the hunter should watch and mark down single birds which may be easier to approach. Rock partridges, like redlegs are somewhat vociferous birds and their calls often betray their presence, especially as the covey tries to regroup.

*Chukar head for comparison*

# European Migratory Quail
## (*Coturnix coturnix*)

THE COMMON, OR MIGRATORY, quail is found as a breeding species across much of Europe, with a few reaching as far north as southern England and even parts of Scandinavia. Moving south in the autumn, the majority over-winter in Africa, although some remain in Spain, Southern Italy and Greece.

The quail is a very small gamebird, approximately half the size of a partridge, with a short, barely visible tail and sandy coloured plumage. Upper parts and flanks are fairly dark, mottled with black and reddish-brown and streaked with buff. The head is striped with buff and brown and the cock has a black stripe running down the middle of the throat.

The chest is marked with spotted streaks – dark brown, and rather more noticeable, in the hen and pale reddish-brown in the cock. Underparts are buff and relatively unmarked.

Quail tend to avoid hedgerows, woodland and rocky areas, favouring a diverse agricultural patchwork of crops, grassland and fallow fields, especially where the land is not intensively farmed. Whilst the breeding population is fairly widespread, climate plays an important part in their choice of habitat with humid conditions preferred over both wet and arid areas. Thick cover is not particularly important as it takes very little to conceal these small and beautifully camouflaged birds. The quail's diet is similar to that of the partridge and includes a wide variety of grain, weed seeds and green material together with insects in the spring, which are important for the breeding condition of the hen.

Quail were once netted and trapped in vast numbers at the migration bottlenecks in Africa and the practice still continues, to a lesser extent, today. However, modern farming practices – the excessive use of herbicides and pesticides in both their winter and summer range – are thought to be responsible for their continued decline. Currently there is no management strategy.

The spring migration occurs in about April, the cocks arriving in small groups ahead of the hens and immediately establishing territories. When the hens arrive, they first seek out suitable nesting sites before responding to the cock's display. Quail are generally monogamous though it is thought that they may, occasionally, be successively polygamous.

The nest is usually sited in weedy or grassy vegetation and 7–14 eggs are laid between

*Cock*

mid-May and late August with the later clutches generally being the result of first nest predation. Incubation and brood rearing is normally by the hen alone. The chicks can make very short flights by about 10 days and fly well by 3 weeks. A high protein diet of insects is essential for the survival of such small chicks but by about 3 weeks they gradually become more vegetarian. The broods break up at 2–3 months, after which the birds become fairly solitary and begin to return to their wintering grounds during September. Relying on their superb camouflage, quail have few major avian predators, other than corvids at the nest, though foxes, weasels and cats etc. are all important.

Shooting begins in mid-September and ends, in most areas, with the autumn migration. Quail sit very tight and are difficult to find and flush without a dog, making them an ideal walked up gamebird for guns with pointers. Flight is slow and low, with fast wingbeats, the birds rarely travelling further than 200 yards before landing in cover. Tending to congregate in areas of good habitat along their migration routes, quail can provide very exciting shooting. They are surprisingly small and easily missed.

*Cock*

# Turtle Dove (STREPTOPELIA TURTUR)

WINTERING IN TROPICAL AFRICA, the turtle dove's summer range extends across Europe as far north as southern Scotland and central Russia. Once common, the population is declining as a result of habitat degradation through modern farming practices. Over-shooting, both of migratory birds in Europe and more resident populations in Africa, is thought by many to be compounding the problem. The turtle dove is easily distinguished from other doves and pigeons by its richly patterned upper parts and black-striped white collar patches. In flight they are sometimes confused with the collared dove, though they are less heavily built and the dark tail is more pointed and edged with white. The call is an unmistakeable dreamy purr.

Turtle doves typically favour diverse farmland, broken up with fairly open broad-leaved or mixed woodland. They prefer woodland edge in which to nest and roost and parkland is ideal whilst dense forests are avoided. Their diet consists of the weeds and weed seeds in arable fields during much of the summer with grain, sunflower seeds and berries becoming increasingly important in autumn.

Arriving in their breeding range in April or May, the turtle doves soon pair and seek out suitable nesting sites. The nest itself is an uncomfortable looking platform of twigs in a tree or bush, usually within about 10ft of the ground. Turtle doves are territorial immediately around the nest and make display flights similar to the woodpigeon. The first clutch of 2 eggs is laid in late May and the pair will usually raise two broods with both parents sharing rearing and incubation duties. As with other doves, the chicks are fed on 'pigeon milk', regurgitated from the adult's crop and the young remain dependent on their parents for a short period after leaving the nest at 18–20 days. Predation of the clearly visible eggs by corvids can be high and both adults and young are easily taken by sparrowhawks and a few other birds of prey.

In September and October, turtle doves gradually head south to their wintering grounds. Along these migration routes, they may congregate in large numbers in areas of good feeding, though they tend to move in small groups rather than large flocks.

Fully protected in the British Isles, the shooting season in the southern part of the continent lasts from the end of August until they have departed and the majority are therefore shot in southern Europe. One of the traditional migration flyways takes them through north-west Africa where the boosted resident population can reach pest proportions.

The vast majority of turtle doves are shot coming into grain and sunflower fields. Whilst pigeon decoys will attract them, they are rarely necessary and the gun generally conceals himself, overlooking a well-used field.

Turtle doves do not tend to gather in large numbers in the evenings to enable roost shooting and, in any event, the leaf cover of the trees would prevent this method. However, waiting for the morning movement along the flight lines between roosting and feeding areas can often be productive and some are also walked up along woodland edges.

# European Elk (ALCES ALCES ALCES)

THE EUROPEAN ELK IS found in Scandinavia, Russia and eastern Poland. There are 4 sub-species in North America, where they are confusingly called moose – elk being the name given to the wapiti – but almost twice as many elk are shot each year in Scandinavia, attracting hunters from all over the world.

Elk are the largest deer in the world, though, standing 5–6ft at the shoulder, the European is a little smaller than the North American sub-species. Their sheer size and ungainly appearance, together with a short neck and pronounced shoulder hump, easily identifies them. The coat is dark brown with greyish or white on the lower legs and the bulls have a loose fold of skin, the 'bell',

*European elk*

hanging from the throat. The bull's antlers are wide spreading and palmated, with points growing from the leading edge. Their eyesight is poor but hearing and scenting abilities are excellent.

Whilst elk can be found in purely coniferous woodland, they prefer natural, mixed forest, with a varied age structure, good shrub layer and swamps, lakes and rivers nearby. Clearings provide a diverse patchwork of habitat types and promote forest regeneration of aspen and willow etc. upon which they browse. Grazing is minimal, being rather difficult with such short necks, and they prefer to wade into water to drink. Elk also feed on aquatic vegetation and can submerge completely to reach food growing on the bottom of lakes and rivers. Conifer shoots are important in winter when they can cause considerable damage to the forest, especially where several have gathered together to feed. Elk are fairly sedentary, though in the northern parts of their range they generally move to lower ground in winter to avoid deep snow.

The rut is in September and October when the bulls wander in search of the cows, fighting and advertising their presence. The dominant

*North American moose for comparison*

bulls generally stay with one cow until mated before moving on to the next. Outside the rut, elk are solitary, except for cows with calves at foot. The bulls shed their antlers between late December and early February – the older animals casting earlier – and the new set are cleaned of velvet in late August–September.

In May or June, cows drop their calves – usually singles or twins, rarely triplets. The calves, sexually mature at about $2\frac{1}{2}$ years, generally remain with their mothers for 12 months before being driven away. Although they are otherwise independent by then, it is essential that they stay with the cow through their first winter to benefit from her snow-ploughing abilities. Predation of both adults and young is mostly by wolves though bears will also take calves.

*Hunting seasons generally fall between September and January.*

The ability to easily remove a carcass is an important consideration when hunting an animal as large as this. North American hunters commonly work from a boat, or drive along the logging roads in the forest, in order to drop the animal as close to their method of transport as possible.

However, in Scandinavia the situation is often more organised, with all-terrain vehicles available to reach the remotest areas. Whilst they are sometimes stalked or called by the hunter, elk are most commonly driven to standing guns or trailed with dogs and shot once the animal is held at bay. The cull is carefully monitored to maintain a valuable and healthy population whilst minimising forest damage. Bulls, cows and calves may be allowed, depending on the cull already achieved, and regulations stipulate that the calf must be shot before the cow. There must also, by law, be a dog available to follow up wounded beasts.

# Eurpoean Mouflon (OVIS MUSIMON)

THE MOUFLON, ORIGINALLY FOUND in Corsica and Sardinia, was introduced into continental Europe during the early 1900s where its range now extends from Portugal to Bulgaria and Greece to Denmark with some even found in Sweden and Finland. Whilst the introduced population is increasing, the indigenous mouflon in Corsica and Sardinia have suffered a severe decline and were, until recently, considered an endangered species.

*Ram in summer*

European mouflon are the smallest of the wild sheep, standing about $2\frac{1}{2}$ ft at the shoulder. The coat is a reddish-brown, darker in winter when the ram has a blackish ruff and a pale, almost white, saddle which all but disappears in summer. The lower legs, rump and underparts are also predominantly white. The ram's horns grow in a tight spiral, almost imperceptibly flaring outwards at the tips – though they have been known to grow into the neck, ultimately killing the animal. Ewes only occasionally carry short horns.

In their natural range, mouflon inhabit mountainous forests. However, the introduced population has adapted to a wide variety of habitat from semi-arid rocky regions, through open mountains to low and hilly forest. Found at lower altitudes than chamois – those in Holland are barely above sea level – there is perhaps a preference for open mixed forest, though they can be found in dense coniferous or deciduous woodland. Seasonal movement is minor as they are seldom high enough or far enough from sheltered cover for snow to become a problem. Whilst they can occasionally cause damage to arable crops,

mouflon tend to feed on areas of grassland within the forest and graze rather more than they browse. They can be fairly active during the day especially in the rut.

The rut runs from October to December and is at its most intense in November. The rams fight agressively to establish dominance as they go in search of the ewes. No harem, as such, is formed though the ewes remain in their herd. Outside the rut, the older rams become fairly solitary or form small bachelor groups whilst the main herds consist of ewes and lambs.

*Ram in winter*

In April or May the ewes drop single lambs (rarely twins) which are able to keep up with the herd almost immediately. Mature at about 18 months, the young rams wander off to join the other males whilst the ewes remain with their mothers' herd.

Mouflon seasons run through the autumn and winter when both rams and ewes are shot. There are some organised driven shoots, especially in Spain and Germany, and drives may also include deer and wild boar. The majority, however, are shot from high seats or stalked, either on the open hill or within the forest. Mouflon are very wary animals, with good eyesight and require much skill to stalk successfully, though the terrain is somewhat easier to negotiate than chamois country.

## *Chamois* (RUPICAPRA RUPICAPRA)

CHAMOIS, CONSIDERED BY BIOLOGISTS to be a goat-antelope, have a wide distribution throughout the mountainous regions of central and southern Europe. The genuine chamois, or 'shammy', leather was once made from the skin of this hardy animal, though it now comes from sheep and goats.

The chamois is a most superbly agile and beautiful animal. The sexes, commonly called bucks and does, are alike and stand about $2\frac{1}{2}$ft at the shoulder though the does are slightly smaller. Chamois have a reddish or pale brown summer coat which becomes very thick and dark brownish-black in winter. A white stripe runs from the forehead to the nose, and the throat, lower jaw, insides of the ears and rump are also white. Both bucks and does carry close set horns which are never cast, grow to about 10 inches and curve back sharply at the tips. The hoofs have rubbery pads which offer sure-footed grip over their rocky terrain.

Chamois are found between 2000 and 8000ft, ranging widely across open rocky ground and alpine pastures in summer and moving down to forested areas in winter, although some may remain in lower areas throughout the year. Active during the day, chamois mostly graze in summer and browse in winter and their diet consists of grasses, weeds, lichens, leaves, conifer shoots, twigs and bark, sometimes causing considerable damage in forestry.

The rut is between the end of October and early December when the bucks establish loose territories. No harem is formed but the bucks pursue and fight for the does, driving off the lesser males, and may often be seen in the company of several females. After the rut the older bucks tend to become fairly solitary whilst the does, young and perhaps one or two yearling bucks herd together (and are usually found on higher ground).

Between mid-May and early June the doe leaves the herd to drop her young – usually one but occasionally twins. The kid is soon able to keep up with the doe and they rejoin the herd within a day or two. The young are sexually mature at 3 years old but the bucks are unlikely to get the chance to breed during their first 7–8 years. Chamois have few major predators mainly because the wolf, bear and lynx are uncommon within their range.

*Winter*

*Summer*

However, mortality can be high in this hostile environment. Skiing activity causes much disturbance, at a time when they need to conserve their energy, and food can be in short supply especially where overgrazing by domestic stock occurs. Casualties are of considerable benefit to the rare lammergeyer, the bone-breaking vulture which cleans up the carcass after the other scavengers have had their fill.

*Hunting seasons generally run from August to December.*

At high densities, chamois are prone to disease and the population therefore needs careful managment. A local guide is essential, not only to lead one safely across the often dangerous ground but also to identify bucks and does and choose a suitable beast. Selection being important, chamois are rarely driven.

Occasionally, high seats are used along a woodland edge or ride but generally chamois are either still-hunted in the forest or spied and stalked on open ground which can be remarkably steep. The danger lies in this difficult terrain, especially after the shot has released the hunter's pent up excitement.

## *Ibex* — SPANISH *(CAPRA PYRENAICA)* & ALPINE *(CAPRA IBEX IBEX)*

THE SPANISH IBEX IS found in mountainous regions from the Pyrenees to extreme southern Spain. The population was once widespread and numerous but, by the early 1900s, the Portuguese ibex had become extinct and the other sub-species were in severe decline, primarily due to over-hunting. In the Pyrenees, the ibex is still endangered whilst the remaining

*Spanish ibex*

*Female alpine ibex*

sub-species have increased dramatically and are stable.

The alpine ibex, found throughout the Alps and particularly in the more arid regions, similarly suffered a huge decline and, by 1800, the total population of about 100 animals was confined to northern Italy. These were strictly protected in the Gran Paradiso National Park, created specifically for them. As they recovered, re-introductions were made across much of their former range and the population is now healthy and increasing.

Of a generally similar appearance, these two wild goats differ mostly in their horns. The slightly smaller Spanish ibex has a reddish-brown coat with darker lines along the back and between the flanks and paler underparts. The long horns have less pronounced ridges and form an open spiral, compared to the outward sweeping curve of the alpine ibex which has a more greyish-brown coat. The females of both have small horns and lack the short beards of the males.

Although occasionally seen in forested

areas, ibex are generally found between the tree and permanent snowlines – a rocky habitat broken by alpine pasture and scrub. Remarkably sure-footed on steep rock faces, they are hardy animals but tend to avoid deep snow and can, therefore, make minor seasonal movements in altitude. Generally active during the day, ibex become more nocturnal with increased disturbance. Grazing and browsing, their diet consists of grasses, lichens and the leaves and shoots of shrubby vegetation.

The rut is in November and December, the males fighting for dominance and mating with several females without forming a harem. Outside the rut, ibex form single sex herds, though the older males often become solitary – resting up during the day in caves or amongst the rocks. Females and young can form herds of up to 100 animals.

Females give birth to single kids, occasionally twins, in April or May and rejoin

*Male alpine ibex*

the herd within a few days. The kids stay with their mothers for about 12 months before the young males disperse to join the bachelor herds. Ibex are generally agile enough in this rocky environment to escape predators but the young may be taken by wolves, lynx and eagles.

Shooting seasons generally fall between September and January though on private, fenced preserves, spring hunting may be allowed. Shooting is strictly controlled with few permits available, probably making ibex the most expensive trophy in Europe.

Most ibex are stalked and the hunter is always accompanied by a local guide, who first spies a suitable beast. Ibex are wary animals with very sharp eyesight and acute hearing and their terrain often necessitates long and difficult stalks and a considerable amount of climbing. On the private reserves, they are sometimes driven and, whilst the trophies are frequently larger, the shooting – stalked or driven – is somewhat easier.

## *W*ild Boar *(SUS SCROFA)*

THE WILD BOAR'S NATURAL range extends throughout most of Europe – although extinct in the British Isles since the late 1600s – and there are introduced populations in parts of Scandinavia. Generally considered to be the ancestor of the domestic pig, the two will cross

and produce fertile offspring. Wild boar are increasing across Europe, though swine fever, often contracted from domestic animals, can cause fluctuations in numbers.

Wild boar stand 2 1/2 – 4ft at the shoulder and their smaller hindquarters give them an instantly recognisable, heavy-fronted

*Tusks*

appearance. The sexes are similar, having a thick dark brown coat of coarse hair which turns greyish in summer, though the boar is larger and his tusks longer. The lower tusks grow continuously and can reach 10 inches or more, a third of which protrudes from the jaw. Both sets grow upwards, the lower tusks being constantly honed against the upper set, and may be concealed by the top lip, unless very long. If an upper tusk should break, it may not grow quickly enough to sharpen and keep the lower tusk in check and such deformations can lead to feeding problems.

Wild boar inhabit thick forest, scrub, farmland and swamps. Offering both cover and food, mixed or deciduous rather than purely coniferous woodland is preferred. They are unlikely to be found above 3000ft and the lowland areas of arable land tend to provide a more varied diet.

Except where completely undisturbed, wild boar lie up in very thick cover during the day and emerge at dusk. The older, warier animals will often wait until after dark and may remain in the forest on moonlit nights. Their enormously varied diet includes forest mast, potatoes, sugar beet, eggs, rabbits, rodents, game poults and carrion. Effectively ploughing the ground with their tusks, as they search for roots in the woods, they improve the soil structure and please the forester. However, they can cause considerable damage to pasture – by turning clumps of earth in their quest for mice – and to crops by feeding, ploughing or simply lying down. Whilst hunters revere the wild boar, farmers continue to regard them as pests.

Wild boar may stay with a particular food supply for several weeks but they are unpredictable in their behaviour and can move great distances, especially when disturbed. After bathing in muddy wallows, they rub against nearby trees but they follow no fixed routine and may desert a favoured wallow or rubbing post for no apparent reason. In groups they are vocal animals, grunting and squealing as they root about for food, and disturbance will send them crashing through the undergrowth. Yet, when the need arises, a single animal will creep about silently. Their cunning and unpredictable nature has,

quite rightly, earned them enormous respect.

The rut is mainly in November and December, though it can extend from October to March. The boars become active during the day, fighting for dominance as they wander in search of the sows with which they mate polygamously. Outside the rut the boars become solitary once more whilst the sows, yearlings and piglets remain in quite social groups.

Between March and May, the sow makes a grassy nest in thick cover and gives birth to 3–9 piglets which she agressively defends. Other than the wolf, they have few predators but, given the chance, the boar would eat the piglets. The family rejoins the group after a week or two and by 6 months the young, having lost their brown and buff stripes, become a dark red which turns brown by a year and darkens thereafter. Independent at 6 months, they remain with the group for about 2 years.

Whilst boars are usually allowed to be shot throughout the year, sows are generally protected between the end of winter and the following autumn, during which time driven shooting also stops. Rifle calibres smaller than 7mm are usually avoided and 9.3mm are the most commonly used.

Stalking is not widely practised but some hunters wait for wild boar, at dusk or under a moon (illegal in some countries), near their feeding grounds, wallows or rubbing posts. Perhaps to disguise their own scent, wild boar are attracted to wallows baited by strong smelling substances such as chocolate or even diesel oil and tar. After wallowing they will move to a rubbing post where the height of the mud will indicate the size of the animal and if it is not dry, then the post is still being used. But they follow no fixed pattern or routine in feeding, wallowing and rubbing. The hunter may have a long wait and the animal may not show up at all.

The vast majority of wild boar, however, are driven. Whilst 2 guns and a beater may take part on an informal day, the big estates can have drives lasting 2–3 hours, covering 2000 acres and involve 120 guns, 50 beaters and 50 dogs, producing a bag of, perhaps, 60 boar. Whilst guns are sometimes placed in high seats, stands are more commonly on the ground and usually sited along traditional boar routes. Safety is of the utmost importance and the guns generally stand against the cover being driven and shoot away from it. Guns should not move under any circumstances, even if a beast has been wounded. Hunters, waiting in eager anticipation, often see what they want to see and any moving object could be mistaken for a boar.

Eventually wild boar will break cover but they are very clever beasts and can show remarkable cunning by creeping to the woodland edge before thundering across a ride or racing away to the next wood. They can move fast and most will only offer running shots. Some people have difficulty in quickly lining up open sights and many are now using 'scopes designed for running game, with low magnification and a special reticle. Whilst they possess keen hearing and scenting abilities, their eyesight is poor and, therefore, guns should stand close in along the edge of cover

to avoid being seen. It is important to remember that these are dangerous animals. The dogs – mostly terriers and other small breeds which can get through the thickest of cover – are frequently injured and boar will often charge towards the sound of the human voice calling them away as they press too close.

Rarely shooting a piece of cover more than twice, a typical syndicate will shoot 4–6 times during the season, although there are some which only organise a second day if the cull is not achieved on the first. Most estates concentrate on culling the younger animals, perhaps imposing a penalty fine if the beast is over 100kg or so, and try to leave the older sows which are able to rear considerably more piglets. Some food and water may be provided but the most important management practice is to leave the woods undisturbed. In some areas wild boar are released for shooting into fenced estates but this practice is now made difficult by legal procedures and is, in any event, not generally necessary.

*Piglets*

# North American
## Quarry Species

NOWADAYS IN THE BRITISH ISLES the cost of game management is largely covered by sold shooting. It is simply too expensive for all but the wealthiest for it to be otherwise and much of our wildlife depends upon it – not just game.

In North America, whilst there are a few hunting preserves on private land, most habitat management is carried out by the state. Game has suffered in the face of man's use of the land, much as it has in Europe, but there have been some remarkable success stories – perhaps due to the fact that, once the habitat has been improved, re-stocking is carried out using wild caught game, translocated from areas of plenty. Hand rearing is minor and generally restricted to private reserves where a certain number of pheasants, for example, are released, to order, on the day. There is very little driven shooting as game is simply not so intensively managed to provide a large enough surplus to warrant it.

Vermin control is generally not practised and, in any event, many of the predators are fully protected or hunted as game in their own right – crows, squirrels, bears, mountain lions etc. – and subject to seasons, bag limits and permit restrictions. The money received from all game permits goes towards wildlife management, while the British buy game licences from the post office and wonder what happens to the fee (although this is currently under review).

The North American quarry list shares very few species with the European other than wildfowl and the enormously varied habitat provides a wealth of game – most noticeably 9 species of grouse, including the ptarmigans, and 6 different quail – and shotguns, rifles, handguns and bows are used by the hunters. The following takes a look at some of the animals and upland gamebirds encountered in Canada and the United States. Hunting seasons vary enormously from state to state and year to year – in poor years some species may be fully protected. Bag limits apply to virtually all quarry species but are again variable from one state to another.

*Cock*

# Ruffed Grouse (BONASA UMBELLUS)

OF THE THREE TIMBER grouse hunted in North America, the ruffed is the most important and has a fairly widespread range in the forested areas of Canada, Alaska and north-eastern and north-western United States.

Amongst the many sub-species there are two main colour phases – red and grey. The markings of both are similar but those with a greyish-brown plumage tend to be found towards the north and on higher ground. This has led to the theoretical explanation that they are offered more camouflage in mixed forest whilst the reddish-brown phase blends more effectively with the leaf litter of deciduous woodland.

Ruffed grouse have fairly long tails with a broad dark sub-terminal band (incomplete at the centre in hens). Apart from reddish-

orange combs above the cock's eyes, the sexes are very similar with mottled and spotted upper parts and barred underparts. The crest is often visible but the dark ruff is usually only raised during display or, to a lesser extent, by the hen in brood defence.

Ruffed grouse inhabit a wide range of forest types, from mixed to deciduous and dry to rain-forest. They prefer young, regenerating woodland and will associate with clearings promoting deciduous growth within blocks of coniferous trees. In summer, ruffed grouse feed on low shrubs, berries and forest mast but arboreal feeding is vital in winter when snow covers the ground.

The cock, having secured a territory

115

*Cock displaying*

keeps it for life and his drumming advertisement, at dawn and dusk, can be heard in
any month, though activity peaks in April and,
to a lesser degree, in the autumn. The
drumming, made by the wings, is usually
performed from the same log or tree stump.

Ruffed grouse are polygamous, though no
harem is formed, and the hens visit the cocks
for mating before May when the territories
tend to break down. The nest is usually made
at the base of a tree or stump and 8–15 eggs
are laid in late April. The young are
independent at about 3 months and the
broods generally break up in mid-September.
Outside the breeding season, hens and young
birds can, very occasionally, be found together
but ruffed grouse are generally solitary birds.

When snow covers the ground ruffed
grouse feed almost exclusively in trees and the
catkins and buds of aspen, birch and poplar
become the most important foods. In summer,
ruffed grouse roost on the ground or in
deciduous trees but as the temperature drops
they resort to conifers and, in hard weather, if
the snow condition permits, they will form
snow holes at night.

There is a fairly predictable 10 year cycle,
closely linked to the cycles of their two main
predators, goshawks and great horned owls,
which in turn result from the snowshoe hare
cycle. Other major predators include bobcats
and coyotes.

The ruffed grouse population is stable in
areas of good forest management. In the
United States they are generally declining as
the forests mature but in Canada, where
woodland management and
forest fires create good
regeneration, the
population is thought
to be stable. There are
some areas where
wildlife and forest

managers are working in co-operation to
improve the habitat.

*Hunting seasons fall between September and
January.*

Whilst the ranges of the two birds only
partially overlap in the east, ruffed grouse and
American woodcock are often hunted
together. Ruffed grouse are walked up and
hold fairly well to pointing dogs before
bursting loudly into flight. With or without a
dog, they are a challenge – the cover is often
very thick, allowing only a brief snap-shot
through the tangled branches and, in flight,
they are remarkably agile amongst the trees.

Wandering aimlessly through the forest is
usually unproductive and experienced hunters
head for stands of young aspens – with a trunk
thickness similar to their wrist – as well as old
deserted orchards and areas along stream
banks with aspen, willow, alder and shrubs.

*Hen*

*Cock spruce grouse*

*Hen*

# Spruce Grouse (DENDRAGAPUS CANADENSIS)

THE SPRUCE GROUSE IS found in the coniferous forests throughout most of Canada and Alaska and some areas in northern United States. Inhabiting country where man rarely ventures, these timber grouse are often remarkably tame and unalarmed by hunters, earning them the name 'fool hen'. As a result, spruce grouse are hunted more for food – often by elk and other big game hunters – than as a sporting quarry. Where they are little hunted it may take thrown sticks to get them to fly and many are shot on the ground or in trees with hand guns and rifles.

The cock is greyish, marked with brown and black, and has a black throat, chest and tail which is tipped with pale reddish-brown (except in the Franklin spruce grouse in parts of the west). The breast and underparts show considerable white flecking and the combs above the eyes are scarlet. In display the neck feathers are ruffled but there is no area of bare skin on the neck and this, combined with the white on the underparts and smaller size, should avoid any confusion with blue grouse. The hen could be mistaken for the blue grouse hen and the ruffed grouse. However, the underparts are more conspicuously barred, the tail shorter and darker and there is no crest as in the ruffed grouse.

Spruce grouse show a preference for fairly young stands of pine and spruce or open forest with mixed aged trees. Between late autumn and early spring their diet consists mostly of the needles of these two trees, with ground foraging of blueberries and cranberries etc. occurring in summer.

Hens obtain separate territories to the cocks and usually lay a clutch of 4–8 eggs close to the base of a tree. Incubation and brood rearing is by the hen alone and the young are independent at about 3 months, the birds thereafter becoming fairly solitary.

The population is thought to be relatively stable except in the south-eastern parts of its range.

# Blue Grouse (DENDRAGAPUS OBSCURUS)

LIKE THE SPRUCE GROUSE, and for the same reason, the blue grouse – largest of the timber grouse – is also called the 'fool hen'. Inhabiting coniferous forest in western United States and Canada, blue grouse are seldom found far from trees.

The cock is a dusky blue with brownish mottled wings and can be distinguished from the spruce grouse by its longer tail – tipped broadly with grey on most subspecies – and white under-tail coverts. The combs above the eyes are generally orange and the flanks are flecked with white.

*Hen*

*Cock*

When displaying the general shape is similar to that of the cock spruce grouse, with the tail fanned and held high, but large areas of pinkish-purple or yellow bare skin are exposed on either side of the neck. The feathers surrounding these air sacks are fanned outwards and their white bases revealed. Hens have a similar mottled and barred appearance to the spruce grouse hen but their underparts are more flecked with white than barred.

During the winter blue grouse are found in the higher coniferous forest, feeding almost exclusively on the needles of firs and hemlocks. In the spring they move down to more open, mixed forest where berry bearing shrubs and other plants provide a more varied diet, though conifer needles remain the most important food item.

The cocks obtain new, or re-establish their old territories in the spring, hooting and posturing in display and territorial advertisement. The hooting, made by inflation of the air sacks, is heard mostly in the mornings and evenings and the hens visit the most impressive cocks for mating only.

The nest is often sited under log piles or fallen trees – though occasionally some distance from tree cover – and the clutch consists of 5–8 eggs. Incubation and brood rearing is by the hen alone and the chicks, flying well at 10–14 days, are relatively independent after only a few weeks. However, they remain together until late August or September and, as autumn progresses, they begin to work their way up to their higher winter range and become rather solitary.

Like the spruce grouse, blue grouse are little hunted as a sporting quarry though they are sometimes walked up, with or without dogs.

*Cock displaying*

*Cock sage grouse displaying*

# Sage Grouse (CENTROCERCUS UROPHASIANUS)

THE SAGE GROUSE, LARGEST of the North American grouse, is found in the sagebrush valleys and plains of the western states and small parts of south-west Canada. Overgrazing caused severe decline between the wars and, although numbers are currently stable, large areas of sagebrush are under threat from the plough and herbicides. The implications of further habitat loss, for a bird so dependent on sagebrush, are plain to see.

Sage grouse are unlikely to be confused with any other bird. The cock has black underparts, white breast and a black throat, bordered thinly with white. The upper parts are fairly dark – marked with black, brown and cream – and there is a yellow comb above the eye. When displaying, the cock raises its sharply pointed tail feathers in a stunning fan; the breast becomes monstrously enlarged, almost enveloping the head, as the greenish-yellow air sacks are exposed, and dark hair-like feathers are erected behind the head. The hen is less striking, having an overall greyish-brown mottled plumage with a black belly, white throat and white eyestripe.

During the winter, sage grouse feed almost exclusively on sagebrush and inhabit areas where this is tall enough to stand clear of the snow and provide cover. As spring approaches they move to more open sagebrush where the leaves and seeds of other vegetation are also eaten.

Sage grouse use leks or strutting grounds to display, arriving in the early spring a week or two before the hens. The dominant cocks, which establish central territories at the strutting grounds, attract most of the hens. Displaying ceases in early summer when the cocks tend to form bachelor flocks.

Nests are usually sited under sagebrush plants and 7–8 eggs are laid in April or May. Nest predation by corvids and coyotes, amongst others, can often be high. The broods tend to break up at about 3 months though hens and young birds pack together in the autumn before moving off to their wintering grounds. During periods of hard weather these packs can be very large but the older cocks tend to remain in smaller single sex groups.

*Most shooting seasons, which may be only a week or two long, fall between late August and November.*

Sage grouse tend to feed during the mornings and afternoons, resting or moving to find water in between. Thus the likely areas can be hunted with some degree of predictability. Dogs are useful as these birds often rely on camouflage to protect them. When flushed, hens rise more easily than cocks which take time to gather momentum. However, sage grouse have a deceptive, rolling flight, their bodies swinging from side to side, and are often missed by guns used to sharp-tailed and pinnated grouse.

# Sharp-tailed Grouse
## (TYMPANUCHUS PHASIANELLUS)

SHARP-TAILED GROUSE ARE found across much of Canada, Alaska and parts of central and western United States. Whilst there may be a little colour variation, the main difference between the 6 sub-species is their geographical location and thus habitat.

Overgrazing and, to a lesser degree, the application of herbicides has caused severe decline in sharp-tailed grouse in many states. However, the situation is being carefully monitored and in much of Canada, at least, where their

*Cock displaying*

habitat has been largely unaffected by man, the population is thought to be stable. Where the habitat has been improved, wild-caught birds are being translocated and there is a little hope.

The sharptail has brown patterned upperparts, spotted with white, and brown v-shaped flecks closely mark the breast and, more sparsely, the buff underparts. The central two tail feathers extend beyond the rest, giving the bird its name though they are in fact blunted. Both sexes have small crests and, apart from the cock's yellow eye comb, are almost identical.

Whilst prairie sharptails inhabit open woodland with large clearings, thick cover and shrubby vegetation, other sub-species prefer semi-desert scrub, grassland or even sandhills, though some woody cover may be used in winter. In autumn sharptails feed on fruiting shrubs and arable foods such as grain, peas and alfalfa. When snow makes ground foraging difficult, they take to the trees feeding on the buds and catkins of birch, aspen and hazel together with the berries of mountain ash and rose etc. Although they will happily sit in trees to feed, they usually roost in thickish, clumped grasses or, in winter, form snow holes. In summer, insects, grasses, clover and flowers feature in their diet and, consequently, there is some movement to a more open habitat in the spring.

Sharptail cocks re-establish their territories at the lek or dancing ground in late February or March, the hens arriving later. The dancing grounds are traditional, providing the cover remains short, and are sited on rough open land, cultivated fields, meadows, marshes or heathland. Dominant cocks defend small central territories, arriving before sunrise and, at the peak of the season, often remain all day. During display the body is held horizontally with the tail vertical and small pink or purple air sacks are exposed at the sides of the neck. With out-stretched wings, the cock proceeds to dance

with drumming feet.

Sharptails are polygamous and the hens generally visit the dominant cock, though no bond or harem is formed. The cock takes no part in incubation or brood rearing and dancing activities gradually cease in June. Nests are often found in brushy cover, though the plains sharptail tends to nest in grassland. About 12 eggs are laid and the hen will re-lay if the nest is predated. The young are virtually independent at 6–8 weeks and the broods break up at about 3 months. Cocks return to the dancing grounds in the autumn, without the hens, and this allows young birds to establish territories for the following spring. As sharptails move back to their winter haunts they often gather into packs.

Although overgrazing has resulted in their decline, sharp-tailed grouse evolved with land that had always been moderately grazed by bison and deer and avoid tall rank stands of grass. Consequently such areas need to be burned from time to time and this, together with restricted grazing is carried out on some large tracts of public land.

*Shooting seasons fall between mid-September and November.*

Sharptails are walked up in grassland, woodland or marshy areas – especially where there is a concentration of food, such as in berry-bearing shrubby areas and stubbles. In September, with the broods still together and the cocks near the leks, they will often hold well to dogs but by October or November the packs will be wilder and flush more readily. Sharptails tend to flush in loose flocks, perhaps strung out over 50–60 yards.

An alternative to walking up is 'feed field shooting' which offers 'pass shooting'. Effectively driven shooting without the beaters, guns wait up in the morning or evening near a well used stubble field and intercept the birds as they fly in to feed.

## Greater Prairie Chicken or Pinnated Grouse

### (TYMPANUCHUS CUPIDO PINNATUS)

THERE ARE THREE SUB-SPECIES of prairie chicken found in North America and a fourth – the heath hen – became extinct in the 1930s. The endangered Attwater prairie chicken is found in tiny isolated pockets in Texas and both the greater and lesser prairie chickens have suffered enormous range constrictions. Once widely distributed across the prairie grasslands of central United States and southern central Canada they are now restricted to scattered

populations – locally stable in central areas, but overall in decline.

The greater prairie chicken's range does not overlap that of the lesser, which is smaller and has closer but paler barring, and consequently there should be no confusion between the two. Greater prairie chickens are extensively barred with buff and dark brown, with pale throats and short dark tails. Both sexes are similar and have inconspicuous crests and long 'pinnae' (slightly shorter in the hen), lying on the back of the neck. Cocks have a yellowish-orange comb above the eye.

In display, the greater prairie chicken raises the pinnae over its lowered head and inflates the yellowish-orange air sacks on the sides of its neck creating a booming sound as the air is expelled. Greater prairie chickens arrive at the lek, or booming ground, in March or April and, in common with other lek-forming grouse, the dominant cocks hold central territories and attract most of the hens. The booming ground is traditional and usually located in slightly elevated, open areas with short grazed grass. Territories begin to break down in June, though the cocks generally remain in small groups near the booming ground for much of the summer. The diet in summer consists of insects and the leaves and seeds of grasses and arable crops.

Nests are usually sited in lightly grazed grassland and 12–14 eggs are laid in April or May. Re-laying may occur if the nest is predated but not if the brood is lost. At 6–8 weeks the broods tend to break up, mixing with others and gathering in flocks of up to 30 or so in autumn and winter, though at feeding sites there may be concentrations of several hundred. Older cocks will often return to certain booming grounds to display and re-establish territories in the autumn. In autumn and winter, greater prairie chickens feed on grain fields, returning to roost in grassland,

and in snow they will readily feed on the buds of aspens and other trees, and form snow holes in which to roost at night.

The decline of the pinnated grouse is mainly due to overgrazing and the loss of native prairie grassland, whether by ploughing or conversion from native to exotic grasses. By returning arable land to grass, re-introducing the tall, but moderately grazed, native grass species and translocating wild-caught birds into this improved habitat, they may be saved from following the extinct heath hen. At present, little management is carried out.

*Shooting seasons fall between September and January (mostly September and October).*

Feed field shooting is probably the more common method of shooting pinnated grouse. The flight lines to their feeding grounds are well recognised routes and a little reconnaissance, together with an early start, should be rewarded with some exciting shooting.

At other times, these grouse are walked up in grassland. Very early in the season they will hold well to a dog but soon become wilder and flush in groups quite readily. Very occasionally guns, hunting pinnated, sharp-tailed or sage grouse, will organise an impromptu drive.

*Displaying*

# Northern Bobwhite Quail

## (COLINUS VIRGINIANUS)

THE NORTHERN BOBWHITE's natural range is effectively the eastern half of North America, extending south into Mexico but barely touching Canada in the north. Isolated populations in the west have been introduced.

This little bird has many sub-species but those in the United States generally have a similar appearance. There is little range overlap with the other quail species and, in any event, the bobwhite is easily identified.

The cock has a white face with a dark hazel cap and eyestripe extending down to an almost black neck and the upper parts are mottled with black, brown and buff. Pale underparts are thinly barred with black and the reddish-brown flanks are effectively streaked with white spots. The hen has a reddish-buff face with a brown cap and eyestripe and the markings are generally more subdued, with less contrast, though following those of the cock.

A well balanced and varied landscape of open woodland, scrub, arable and grassland offers the ideal habitat, with little seasonal movement necessary. Insects form an important part of the diet in the breeding season, together with green weedy material, and during the autumn they become increasingly dependent on weed seeds, grain, forest mast, fruits and berries. Bobwhites generally feed in the early morning and late afternoon, returning to woody cover in between. They usually roost near the feeding site in cover ranging from stubble to brushy or wooded areas.

There is a general dispersal from woody cover to grassland in the spring and coveys break up towards the end of April, though the pairs may have already formed within the group. Bobwhites are not territorial, though unpaired cocks may sing to advertise their presence.

The nest, a scrape in the ground lined with dead grasses, is found in fairly thick grassland and a first clutch of 14 eggs is laid in April or May, though re-nesting can occur through to September. Whilst some make monogamous pairings, many hens are promiscuous, turning the first clutch over for the cock to incubate before seeking out another mate. Sometimes the hen hatches and rears the brood to about 2 weeks, leaves them to fend for themselves, and re-nests. Furthermore, there have been instances of a hen hatching the first brood, abandoning them at two weeks, re-nesting and leaving the eggs for the cock before laying a third clutch for herself to incubate.

With cold weather and predation by owls, hawks and numerous mammals, including man, the bobwhite has a life expectancy of one year, at best. Indeed, the annual survival rate can be as low as 6%, which perhaps explains such persistant nesting habits.

The young chicks fly at 7–10 days, reach adult plumage at about 10 weeks and are fully grown at 16–20 weeks. As autumn progresses the broods mix with other coveys in what is called the 'fall shuffle'. This interchange of family members avoids the risk of inbreeding and allows unmated and broodless birds to join a covey and thus benefit from vital roosting warmth. Bobwhites do not form snow holes at night and the optimum size of a covey, for maintaining warmth in cold weather, is thought to be 12–15 – enabling them to roost in an outward facing circle with their tails and bodies touching.

*Shooting seasons fall between October and March.*

The bobwhite's winter range of 15–50 acres allows known coveys to be walked up with a certain degree of predictability. However, they

*Cock and hen*

*Bobwhite cock*

can sit very tight and dogless guns may pass the squatting birds within a few feet. Pointers are therefore ideal for hunting bobwhites.

The common practice, after the hurried shots at the erupting covey, is to mark the single birds down and hunt them individually. Guns without dogs sometimes use whistles to imitate and prompt response calls from these birds which are keen to regather. However, whether used for hunting or not, dogs should always be available to retrieve such small and well camouflaged birds.

Still practised in a few places – especially at field trials, where large acreages are covered – is the traditional method of using horses to reach the areas where coveys are expected to be found. There the guns dismount and the dogs are sent ahead to quarter the ground.

# California Quail
## (CALLIPEPLA CALIFORNICUS)

THERE ARE 5 SPECIES of quail found in western parts of North America: California, mountain, Gambel's, scaled and Montezuma. Whilst the others are locally important, the California, or valley quail, is the most extensively hunted. Originally found in California and bordering states, introductions have led to its current range from extreme south west Canada in the north to the tip of Baja California in the south and inland to Colorado, together with some other parts of the world. The California quail is increasing in British Columbia and stable elsewhere, following significant declines in the 1960s.

The California quail is only likely to be confused with the Gambel's with which it has been known to hybridize in the small area where their ranges overlap. Both cock birds have heavy-looking plumed crests, greyish-

brown plumage and black faces edged with
white. The California, however, has a pale
forehead, not black; the white-streaked flanks
are brownish, instead of chestnut, and the
underparts have a scaled effect and a chestnut,
rather than black, belly patch. The hens have
smaller crests than cocks and the California is
told from the Gambel's by the scaled
underparts.

California quail can be found in habitat
ranging from desert scrub to farmland but
they are dependent on the availability of water,
which they need
to drink every
day in order to
survive. They show
a preference for cattle
and sheep rangeland –
providing it is not
overgrazed – though
deserts offering food,
water and cover are
also important. Dense

shrubby areas, vineyards, sagebrush and
overgrown riverbanks provide escape cover
and roosting – unlike most of the other quail,
the California roosts in trees and shrubs. Their
diet consists almost entirely of the leaves and
seeds of weeds, grasses and native legumes,
although insects are beneficial to breeding
hens in the spring.

California quail begin to pair towards the
end of winter and the coveys break up in late
February or early March, as the unpaired
cocks are chased away. These single cocks
hold loose territories, close to the nests of
other pairs, and are thought to occasionally act
as foster parents to broods where the cock has
been lost.

The nest is a well concealed grass-lined
scrape in fairly thick grassy vegetation. The
12–16 eggs are laid between April and June
though hens will re-lay repeatedly in the event
of nest predation and, to a lesser extent, brood
loss. If the conditions are favourable, hens
occasionally produce 2 broods – the cock

*Gambel's quail for comparison*

taking charge of the first at about 2 weeks whilst the hen incubates the second clutch. Cocks can be polygamous though they will only father one brood at a time. Persistent renesting offsets the effects of predation by weasels, skunks, raccoons, hawks, owls and snakes etc., which can be high amongst nesting hens and results consistantly in an excess of cocks in the autumn and winter populations.

The chicks can fly at 10–14 days, during which time insects are crucial to their survival. Adult plumage is attained at about 10 weeks

and in late summer the family groups, both pre-flight and almost full grown, begin to merge in the 'fall shuffle'. Winter coveys can be large – 100–200 or more in favourable habitat towards the south – and generally stay together until the spring, though they can mix occasionally. The establishment of a pecking order is thought to explain fighting within the covey.

Management practices generally involve the provision of water and the creation of different habitat types through burning brush and scrub and discing strips of land to encourage certain preferred weeds.

*Shooting seasons fall between October and January.*

Like the bobwhite, California quail are walked up and generally hold well to pointing

dogs. The method of following up the scattered single birds after the covey has flushed is also practised and the experienced guns hunt around water holes, streambanks (especially those bordering grainfields) and oak-woodland edge.

# Wild Turkey (MELEAGRIS GALLOPAVO)

THE WILD TURKEY IS NOW found and hunted in every American state (except Alaska), as well as Mexico and even one or two Canadian provinces, though populations to the north and west were introduced.

There are 5 North American sub-species: the eastern, which is probably the most common, Florida, Merriam's, Rio Grande and Gould's. A sixth, called the Mexican or ocellated turkey, is found in Central America and is the original ancestor of the domestic turkey.

Whilst there are colour variations between the sub-species, their general shape is similar and it is impossible to confuse them with any other bird. The sexes resemble each other, though the hen is more subdued in plumage

*Hen*

and facial colour and is somewhat smaller than the mature male, which is called a tom or gobbler. The beard – a tuft of hair-like feathers sprouting from the chest – continues to grow throughout the gobbler's life but is only seen occasionally in the hen. The blue, bare-skinned, head is covered with pinkish growths and throat wattles.

Turkeys favour deciduous or mixed forest, with a varied age structure, broken up by clearings and agricultural land. They feed on weed seeds, green vegetation, arable crops, insects, forest mast and berries. In snow, they rely on areas cleared by deer or feed near springs where the snow is patchy. In very hard weather they may remain in the trees for several days, feeding on buds.

Habitat loss between the end of the 19th century and the 1930s caused severe declines but reforestation resulted in an excellent recovery. Continued forest management – retaining a diverse age range of trees, clearing areas to allow regeneration and, perhaps, planting fruiting and berry-bearing shrubs – will keep the population healthy.

Gobblers set up territories in April-mid-May, strutting and displaying to attract a harem of hens. Boundary disputes are common but fights are not usually fatal. The nest is situated in shrubby and grassy vegetation and the eggs are laid in late March-June with re-nesting occurring if the eggs are predated. Young hens will lay 8–10 eggs whilst the older birds can produce 16–18. Gobblers play no part in incubation or brood rearing and folklore suggests they will even destroy nests, though this is unproved and, generally, not a belief shared by the biologists. Predators of the nest include raccoons, skunks, foxes and coyotes whilst cougars, bears, great horned owls and golden eagles will take adult birds.

The chicks' diet consists mainly of insects for the first 4–6 weeks. They make short flights at 14–20 days and begin to roost off the ground at about 5 weeks. Hens breed by 12 months but the young males, called jakes, are rarely sexually mature before their second year. Young hens stay with the mother for the first year, joined by other hens and broods in the autumn but the jakes begin to move away in January or February. The adult gobblers, which have remained fairly solitary throughout the summer, will start to band together in bachelor groups during the autumn, rarely mixing with the hens.

*Gobbler displaying*

Most states allow spring gobbler hunting. Whilst this is aimed at territorial birds, the older gobblers are extremely wary and it is frequently the younger and lesser males which respond to the call. During the autumn, both sexes may be shot except in a few states which offer hens full protection.

The classic hunting method is to flush the turkey flock and then try to call them back to re-group. However, much depends on the hunter's patience, camouflage, skills with the calls and ability to locate the birds in the first place. It is an art form, requiring far more than marksmanship. Indeed, the skill is in making the shot as easy as possible. Flying

*Gobbler*

shots are unwise and increase the chance of wounding – they can run very fast and most states will not allow dogs to be used on turkey hunts. The bird should be taken on the ground with a head shot.

*Gobbler*

Other hunting methods involve waiting up near feeding or dusting sites and creeping through the woods in an attempt to surprise a flock, though invariably it is the hunter who is surprised and lucky to catch the briefest glimpse. The use of rifles and the practice of shooting the birds out of their roosts is frowned upon by most turkey hunters, though legal in some states.

Turkey hunting can be quite dangerous: the camouflaged hunter sits very still, possibly having set up a decoy (allowed in some states) and it is likely that there are turkeys nearby. It is certainly possible that others may be hunting the same birds and either mistake the decoy for a live bird or take a shot at the real thing, unaware of the other hunter's presence directly in the line of fire.

# *American Woodcock* (SCOLOPAX MINOR)

THE AMERICAN WOODCOCK IS found in the eastern half of North America – from Florida to southern Canada – both as a migratory bird and a resident, breeding across much of its range and wintering in the more southerly states.

Although very similar in appearance to its European counterpart, the American woodcock is much smaller, only marginally longer than the common snipe. However, it retains the typical dumpy shape, making it quite unmistakable. The colour and general markings closely resemble those of the European woodcock, though the rich pattern on the upper parts is broken up with prominent and clearly defined greyish-buff stripes, edging the scapulars. The underparts are yellowish-buff, lacking the fine barring of the European bird, and the primaries are greyish and unmarked.

Woodcock inhabit damp woodland and boggy thickets by day and flight out to feed on nearby pasture at dusk, probing soft ground with their long bills to reach worms and other invertebrates. They prefer early successional deciduous forest with clearings and rides to provide good edge habitat as well as access and escape routes. Dense shrubby vegetation offers protection from predators such as hawks, owls, coyotes, foxes, mink, weasels and bobcats. The

American woodcock is thought to be stable in central areas but declining in the east.

The migrating woodcock head north to their breeding grounds in March or April, though resident males may be seen displaying as early as February, continuing through to early April. Dominant males fly out to their singing grounds at dawn and dusk. After calling on the ground, the bird rises, circling upwards to several hundred feet with twittering wings before descending in steep steps, almost to the point where the display began. Woodcock are polygamous and the females fly in to the singing ground of the chosen male to mate. The male plays no part in incubation or brood-rearing.

Nesting habits are similar to those of the European woodcock with a clutch of 4 eggs, generally laid in late March or April. The young can fly at 10–14 days and are able to care for themselves within a few weeks. Broods can break up after little more than a month and the birds become fairly solitary, returning to their wintering grounds in October and November.

Shooting seasons fall between mid-September and mid-February. During the autumn, many coverts are annually blessed with transitory falls of woodcock. Hunters concentrate along these traditional migration routes where high numbers of birds can be found before the colder weather pushes them further south.

Where their range overlaps in the east, woodcock and ruffed grouse are often hunted together and occasionally a bobwhite hunter may add a woodcock to his bag. Sitting fairly tight, they are usually walked up over pointing dogs amongst thickets, woodland edges and overgrown orchards. The American woodcock, like the European, invariably flushes when the gun is completely entangled in thick cover and weaves its tantalising way through the trees.

# Mourning Dove (ZENAIDA MACROURA)

THE MOURNING DOVE IS the most widespread and abundant North American gamebird and is frequently encountered in towns and cities as well as in the countryside. They are migratory birds, breeding across the United States, southern Canada and Mexico, though many remain in the more southerly states throughout the year.

It is unlikely to be confused with any other bird except, perhaps, the white-winged dove which inhabits the dry lands and deserts of the south. However, whilst the two are similar facially, the whitewing has a heavier build with a shorter, blunted tail and highly visible white patches on its wings. The mourning dove is a pinkish-buff with greyish-brown upper parts and a few dark spots on the wing coverts. The tail, which is long and pointed, most easily identifies this bird both in the air and on the ground.

In the countryside, the mourning dove favours a patchwork of good agriculture, woodland and hedgerows – a balance which provides feeding, roosting and nesting habitat. Their diet consists of weeds and weed seeds, sunflowers and grain such as wheat, maize, sorghum and millet.

*White-winged dove*

*Mourning dove*

The migrating mourning doves arrive in their breeding grounds between mid-March and early April – the males arriving ahead of the females to set up a territory. Nests are sited in trees, bushes or even on the ground and up to 5 clutches of 2 eggs can be laid, though in the north there may only be 1 or 2 broods before the return migration in late August. Both parents help to incubate and rear the brood, continuing to feed the young with regurgitated food for a short while after they leave the nest at 15–18 days. Squirrels and jays are important predators at the nest, whilst great horned owls and other birds of prey take newly fledged and adult birds.

*Shooting seasons generally fall between September and mid-January, sometimes with a break in the middle.*

Feeding flocks of 15,000 mourning doves are not unknown in some areas outside the breeding season, though small groups and even single birds are often encountered. Whilst such concentrations can cause immense crop damage, some states clasify mourning doves as song birds, offering full protection throughout the year, and all other states set seasons and bag limits – usually 10–12 per day. Despite this, the mourning dove is the most extensively hunted bird in North America – though the white-winged dove and band-tailed pigeon are locally important to the south and west respectively.

Decoys are often used to attract doves into grainfields or weedy areas though they are not always necessary where the birds are regularly using a particular food supply, especially if several hunters are surrounding the field. Similarly, guns may wait up near ponds, streams or even livestock tanks. Doves visit water holes daily, usually in late afternoon, and provide exciting shooting as they flight in, twisting and turning. A bag limit of doves is often referred to as 'a box of shells'.

In the early part of the season, mourning doves will flush a few at a time from standing crops and brushy areas, enabling them to be walked up. It is the hardest and least successful way to shoot them and becomes less productive as the season progresses.

*Band-tailed pigeon*

Some crops are planted and left specifically for doves – usually millet, sunflowers, buckwheat or popcorn. However, it is illegal to bait fields by returning grain that has already been harvested.

*Mourning dove*

# *Wapiti* (*CERVUS ELAPHUS*)

THE WAPITI WAS MISTAKENLY called elk by the early settlers in North America, who confused this large deer with the European elk, and it is still commonly referred to by that name – the real elk subsequently became known as the moose. Wapiti – an Indian word referring to the pale winter coat – are generally considered to be of the same species as the red deer.

At one time widespread almost throughout the United States and southern Canada, wapiti were subjected to much over-hunting until the early 1900s. With re-introductions, careful management and hunting controls, the population is secure and wapiti today are encountered in the western parts of their former range and in isolated pockets across North America. The population is now at its highest since 1800.

Considerably larger than the Scottish red deer, the two most noticeably differ in winter. The wapiti has a pale reddish or greyish-brown winter coat, with dark brown legs, neck and head and a yellowish rump. In summer the coat becomes reddish-brown,

*Caribou for comparison*

similar to that of the red deer. The bull's antlers, like those of the red stag, are wide spreading and generally follow a similar pattern, though there is usually a fourth (dagger or royal) tine and the crown is often less clustered. Their general build, size, colour and antler formation should easily distinguish wapiti from caribou (reindeer) and, indeed, all other North American deer.

Wapiti generally inhabit mountainous coniferous forest, moving to lower ground bordering agricultural land in winter. They are crepuscular, usually lying up in the forest during the day and feeding out into grassland at dusk, though they may spend the summer in alpine meadows above the timberline. Both browsing and grazing, their diet is highly variable and consists of grasses and the leaves and shoots of shrubs and trees.

The rut takes place in September-mid-October, the bulls fighting to gather harems of up to 40 cows. Not

*Wapiti bull in winter*

surprisingly, fatalities sometimes occur and the bulls can suffer enormous weight loss in the process of defending the harem. The speed of recovery usually depends on the severity of the winter. Antlers are cast in March or early April and the new set are clean of velvet in August. Outside the rut, the older bulls become fairly solitary or form small bachelor groups.

The calves – usually singles and very rarely twins – are born in May or June and join their mothers' herd as soon as they are able to keep up. The young often remain with the cow until after the next year's calf is born and generally reach sexual maturity at about 18 months. However, the bull may not reach adult body weight for 7 years or more, the antlers becoming fully developed at 9–10 years old. During the winter, cows, yearlings and calves can often be encountered in herds of several hundred. Predation by coyotes, wolves and bears can be a major limiting factor – wolves and bears taking both calves and adults.

Hunting seasons are generally in the autumn and early winter, though marauding deer on farmland may be shot outside the season. High seats are rarely used and wapiti are usually still-hunted or stalked, both in the forest and on open ground above the timberline.

# White-tailed Deer
## (ODOCOILEUS VIRGINIANUS)

THE WHITE-TAILED DEER is the most abundant and widespread big game animal in North America. Found in southern Canada and most of the United States – except the extreme south-west – their range also extends into northern parts of South America.

There are many sub-species but, generally, the difference in appearance is in body and antler size, with the larger animals to the north and smaller to the south – excepting some introduced herds. Whitetails stand about 3ft at the shoulder, the does being somewhat smaller. The shorter reddish-brown summer coat turns greyish-brown in late autumn and the underparts and underside of the tail are white. White also surrounds the eyes and black nose and there is a white patch on the throat.

The whitetail buck's antlers consist of a main, forward curving beam out of which grow a series of unforked tines. This distinguishes

*Doe*

*Whitetail buck, antlers recently cast*

it from the mule and black-tailed bucks whose antlers branch along the main beam with each tine forking again. In flight, the whitetail leaps and bounces gracefully, the tail held high, flashing the white underside. The mule deer, by comparison, has a black-tipped white tail which is held low during its stiff-legged run.

White-tailed deer prefer a balanced habitat of brushy, wooded areas and farmland. Population density is greater in areas of deciduous woodland though this is due more to the climate than food quality. Whitetails are both browsers and grazers eating a wide variety of foods – forest mast, berries, leaves, twigs, crops, grasses and other vegetation. They can

live in close proximity to man and the 'urban deer' is becoming a major problem. Like all deer, they are excellent swimmers and have been known to cross 7 miles of open water.

By the turn of the century, due to hunting pressure and habitat loss, the whitetail population was in severe decline. Since then, conservation and restricted hunting practices have led to a remarkable recovery – the total population thought to be approaching 30 million. Whitetails are still increasing and moving back into areas they originally inhabited. Their main enemies are coyotes, humans and cars and, to a lesser degree – due to their small numbers – wolves and mountain lions.

*White-tailed buck*

The rut occurs between October and December, though in the south it can continue into January. Bucks do not use rutting stands or take territories but will defend an area around the doe before mating and moving on to find another. Antlers are cast in January and the new set are cleaned of velvet in August and September. Outside the rut, younger bucks are generally found in small, loose groups of 2 or 3, whilst the older animals are often solitary.

In May or June the doe gives birth to her spotted fawns – usually twins but occasionally singles or triplets – which remain hidden until they are able to keep up with her. They are independent at 7–8 months and full grown at about 4 years. Young does may stay with the mother for 12 months, by which time they are, themselves, sexually mature. However, the yearling bucks, which show two spikes, will not get the chance to breed until at least 2 years old.

The family group may come together with others when feeding but otherwise, except in more open habitat, there is little herding. Whitetails are most active at dawn and dusk, possibly becoming more diurnal in areas of little hunting pressure. In the north there is usually some seasonal movement to lower, wetland areas to avoid deep snows and harsh winter conditions. In more southerly regions, however, they have a home range of about 500 acres.

Hunting seasons generally fall between early September and late December. In some states with a large human population, hunting with rifles is illegal and deer may only be taken with shotguns and solid-slug cartridges or, in some areas, buckshot.

The most common hunting practice is 'stand shooting' – using high seats or ground blinds sited along well-used deer tracks, woodland edges or arable land. To a lesser extent, whitetails are stalked in woodland or driven from it, though this latter method is illegal in some states. Hunters often rattle antlers together and use calls to draw the bucks closer but the older animals become very wary, cunning and elusive.

# Mule Deer (ODOCOILEUS HERMIONUS)

MULE DEER ARE FOUND in the western half of the United States, south-west Canada and parts of Mexico. The black-tailed deer, a sub-species, inhabits the extreme west of this range, along the Pacific coast, though they can mix during the summer in mountainous regions.

Generally a little larger than the whitetail, the mule deer's summer coat is yellowish to reddish-brown, turning greyish in winter. A dark fore-head, white rump and black-tipped white tail are the most obvious distin-guishing marks. However, a sub-species to the south has a smaller rump patch and less white on the tail and the black-tailed deer's tail is, as its name implies, completely black above. Antlers,

*Mule deer antlers*

branching along the main beam with the tines forking again, typically reach a maximum of 10 points including the brow tines. Mule deer run with big, stiff-legged, springing bounds and do not raise their tails.

Mule deer habitat varies according to the geographical location of the different sub-species – ranging from mountainous regions, through prairie grassland to semi-desert. They generally prefer more open or brushy areas

*Does*

than whitetails though some do inhabit forest. They are crepuscular – usually resting during the middle of the day and at night – browsing and, to a lesser extent, grazing on a wide variety of vegetation. The plains' mule deer generally have a fairly small home range whilst those in the mountains make seasonal movements in altitude.

Like the whitetail, mule deer once suffered dramatic declines, resulting from habitat loss and over-hunting, but have increased greatly since the early 1900s. The population is thought to be secure though there is some concern over the advancing whitetails and hybridization between the two species.

The rut is between October and December and the swollen-necked bucks, fighting for dominance, are seldom very far from the does,

which visit for mating only. Outside the breeding season, the bucks become solitary or form small bachelor groups of 2–4 though occasionally the sexes mix. Antlers are cast in January or February and the new set are cleaned of velvet in August.

Fawns, usually singles or twins and rarely triplets, are born between April (in the south) and June. Independent at about 8 months, the young tend to leave the does at 9–12 months though family groups of does, yearlings and fawns are sometimes seen.

Hunting seasons are in the autumn and early winter. Generally all states within the mule deer's range allow bucks to be shot. A special permit is usually required for does though some states offer a 2 day doe season.

In the mule deer's more typical treeless habitat, hunters are generally not able to use high seats. However, waiting up in cover near a well used track or feeding area is often productive, both at dawn and dusk.

*Buck*

Reconnaissance is essential, as with all deer hunting, to understand the movements of individual animals and thus improve one's chances.

Alternatively, mule deer are hunted along the lines of open-hill stalking though they are often spied first from a vehicle – the hunters driving along dirt tracks in likely areas. Shots are generally longer than with stand shooting as the cover is often too sparse to allow a close approach.

# *P*ronghorn (ANTILOCAPRA AMERICANA)

THE PRONGHORN IS CALLED an antelope by some and a goat by others. However, although the generic name implies it is a cross between the two, it is neither antelope nor goat but the sole surviving member of a family which originated in North America. Its range extends from central southern Canada, through much of the western half of the United States and into parts of Mexico.

Standing approximately 3ft at the shoulder, the pronghorn is a graceful but powerfully built ruminant. Living out in the open, it relies on speed rather than cover for protection and, reaching 60mph, it is the fastest animal in North America.

The pronghorn has a tan coloured coat with white underparts and a large white rump patch. The buck has a dark facial mask – tan in the doe – with white cheeks and chin and the horns are about 12 inches long, curving back and slightly inwards at the tips, with a small forward pointing fork halfway up. Does usually develop unbranched horns of about $2\frac{1}{2}$ inches in their second year. The horn consists of a central core, covered with an outer sheath which is shed each year, pushed off by the new one growing underneath. Their eyesight is quite outstanding and thought to be the equivalent of 10x binoculars with a zoom feature. Unique among North American ungulates, the pronghorn has only two toes on each foot.

Inhabiting open prairie grassland and desert scrub, pronghorn are virtually never seen in cover, often preferring to run round a wooded ravine rather than through the middle of it. Browsing a little more than

*Buck and doe*

137

grazing, their diet consists of flowering broadleaved shrubs and grassy vegetation. Cattle ranges, where the grass is grazed and the browse remains untouched, provide an excellent habitat. The barbed wire fencing offers little obstruction to the pronghorn which prefers to crawl underneath obstacles – very rarely jumping them – though the bottom strand must be high enough to allow this access. Sheep compete with pronghorn for food and the netting fences severely restrict their movements. They are active throughout most of the day though they tend to lie up and chew the cud between late morning and mid-afternoon. There is little seasonal movement, except in the Rocky Mountains, though they do not scrape through deep snow to reach food and may wander far in search of areas cleared by the wind.

Due to habitat loss and overhunting, the population – thought to have once been about 35 million – declined to about 20,000 by the early 1900s. However, a decline in the human population in the Great Plains has resulted in a considerable reduction of both grazing pressure and agricultural production. Together with hunting restrictions, the pronghorn has recovered to over 500,000 and is increasing. Management practices involve the provision of waterholes and a high proportion of preferred browse within their habitat.

The rut is in September and October when the bucks may become territorial, although this varies between both years and areas. There can be a considerable amount of fighting as they try to gather harems of up to 15 does. Harems break up after mating and, as winter approaches, pronghorn start to form mixed herds of up to 100. During spring and summer these fragment into smaller parties, the mated bucks often forming bachelor groups.

The young, usually twins, are born between late May and mid-June, the doe becoming solitary until they are able to keep up. Leaving their mother at about 10 months, the young bucks and does are sexually mature at 18 months and full grown at 4–5 years. Due to the unrivalled speed of the adults, predation by coyotes, bobcats and golden eagles is mostly of the young.

Hunted in the autumn, pronghorn are mainly stalked across open country, using the folds in the ground for concealment. The problem is not in shooting any animal but in stalking a chosen beast without spooking the whole herd. It is illegal to shoot them from a vehicle though hunters sometimes push a herd to a more approachable position and, after letting them settle, drive round to begin the stalk with the wind in their faces.

Hunters may wait up behind a haystack, or blind, near a well-used waterhole or, though little practised now, place a flag in the ground to attract these inquisitive animals within range.

# *Bighorn Sheep* (*OVIS CANADENSIS*)

THE 6 SUB-SPECIES OF bighorn sheep in North America are broadly categorised into 3 groups: Rocky Mountain, California and desert. Their range extends through much of western United States and Canada, from British Columbia and Alberta in the north to Baja California and northern Mexico in the south. The Rocky Mountain and California bighorns are found in the northern half of this range, with the desert bighorn to the south, although populations in central parts are fairly isolated.

The bighorn suffered a serious decline up until the early 1900s due, partly, to the fragmentation of their habitat by urbanization together with over-hunting but more importantly to grazing competion and pneumonia contracted from domestic sheep. By fencing out livestock, burning to prevent forest regeneration and translocating animals to these improved areas, the bighorn is now carefully managed and restricted hunting has led to a healthy and steadily increasing population, especially with Rocky Mountain and desert bighorns. Re-introductions continue and the outlook is good.

The Rocky Mountain bighorn ram stands about $3^{1}/_{2}$ – 4ft at the shoulder, the desert being somewhat smaller as are the ewes of both. The coat is a darker greyish-brown than that of the desert bighorn but both show a large white rump patch with a fairly small dark tail and the muzzle and chin are white. The ram's horns are large and on a mature Rocky Mountain bighorn they form a tight spiral whilst those of the desert ram have a more open curl. The horns are never shed and the rings represent each year's growth. Ewes produce short curved horns, up to about 10–12 inches long and some confusion may arise between ewes and young rams. Bighorns have rubbery pads on their hoofs to provide a sure grip on slippery surfaces and they are remarkably agile amongst their rocky terrain. There is possibly some overlap between the subspecies where they may well interbreed for they will cross with domestic sheep.

Rocky Mountain bighorn are found in mountainous areas, generally above the timberline but occasionally in open forest, whilst the desert subspecies inhabits open scrubland. Most importantly, they require snow-free grassland close to steep terrain such as rocky mountainsides or river canyons to allow escape from predators – wolves, cougars, bears, coyotes and eagles. The bighorn's diet consists mostly of grasses but they will browse, especially as winter approaches, and, in the desert bighorn's range where there is little

grass, the leaves and shoots of shrubs become increasingly important and the availability of water is essential. In deep snow, bighorn move to areas of ground cleared by the wind. They are diurnal and rest at night in the open, avoiding brushy areas where predators could make a stealthy approach.

The rut runs from July to December in the south with desert bighorn but is generally restricted to November and December in more northerly areas. Bighorn, forming no harem, are promiscuous and there can be a considerable amount of fighting over the ewes. The rams charge each other with their heads lowered, cracking horns together – a sound which may be heard a mile away. The fights can sometimes last a few hours and their horns frequently become chipped. However, previous fights within the bachelor herds, found outside the rut, which establish the hierarchy, may mean the dominant rams mate with the ewes virtually unchallenged.

Desert bighorn lambs are born between January and June or in April – June with the Rocky Mountain sub-species. Single lambs are most common but occasionally there may be twins. Once the lamb is able to keep up with the ewe, they rejoin the nursery herd. The young sheep are independent by the autumn but remain with the nursery herd for 2–4 years when the rams leave to join the bachelor groups. Where the population is expanding, however, the rams may reach sexual maturity by 18 months. There can be some dominance behaviour within the nursery group but it is generally more subtle than the terrifying clashes in the ram herds.

*Hunting seasons are generally in the autumn and early winter.*

Whilst some desert sheep are shot by hunters waiting up at their water-holes, most bighorn are stalked. The majority are shot as only granted one permit in a lifetime and these may only be offered to residents. However, some consider, at least with the Rocky Mountain bighorn, that it is important to control the nursery herds by hunting to avoid over-population of a fairly limited habitat.

There are some dedicated hunters who spend their lives in pursuit of the North American sheep and a 'grand slam' is achieved when all the sub-species of both bighorn and thinhorn have been taken.

*Rocky mountain bighorn*

trophies, the suitable animal having been spied first amongst a herd of watchful eyes. Bighorn possess very keen eyesight and the terrain usually ensures long and difficult stalks in a fairly coverless habitat with a considerable amount of climbing involved.

Some states offer permits for any age rams as well as ewes but generally there are very strict controls. In some desert bighorn states the hunters are

*Desert bighorn ram and ewe*

*Dall's sheep*

# Thinhorn Sheep (OVIS DALLI)

THERE ARE TWO SUB-SPECIES of thinhorn found in North America: Dall's *(Ovis dalli dalli)* and Stone's *(Ovis dalli stonei)*. Both inhabit the mountains of the extreme north-west – the Dall's ranging across parts of British Columbia, Yukon and Northwest Territories and into Alaska, with the Stone's a little to the south in British Columbia and Yukon Territory. In such

remote areas their habitat is unaffected by man but populations may fluctuate enormously as a result of severe winter weather.

Found further north than the bighorn, thinhorn are easily identified. Dall's sheep are white but are unlikely to be confused with the distinctly goat-like white American mountain goat, except perhaps at very long distances. Stone's sheep are generally dark greyish-brown with a paler grey face and neck and white on the muzzle, rump, belly and backs of the legs. However, the Stone's can show remarkable variation and there is an occasional overlap between the ranges of both subspecies. The two will interbreed to produce intermediate colour phases. Body size is a little smaller than the bighorn and the horns are noticeably thinner and taper to fine outward-flaring points in older rams. The ewes possess short horns.

Thinhorn generally inhabit high alpine meadows below the permanent snow line, although the Stone's sheep can often be found

*Stone's sheep*

in somewhat lower country. Like the bighorn they require nearby escape terrain in the form of cliffs and rocky outcrops where they can usually outrun and out-climb predators. Predation is mostly by wolves and coyotes and, to a lesser extent, black and brown bears, eagles, lynx and wolverines. As a rule, thinhorn are mostly diurnal although they must feed at 'night' in the arctic winter with 24 hours of darkness.

The rut generally runs from mid-November to mid-December or possibly a little later with Stone's sheep. Dominance has often already been established amongst the ram herds but they will occasionally fight directly over the ewes. Rams mate promiscuously, without forming a harem. After the rut, the older rams occasionally become solitary but usually form bachelor groups, whilst the younger animals may sometimes be encountered in mixed herds.

The single lambs – very rarely twins – are born between mid-May and mid-June. Once the young are able to keep up, they return to the nursery herd although sometimes the ewe, yearling and lamb may remain as a separate family group. It appears that sexual maturity is reached with adult body weight and varies between 18 months and 4 years, depending on the quality of their feeding. The hierarchy amongst the ram herds means that the males are unlikely to breed before 3–4 years old, and even then their contribution will be minor unless the older rams have been removed. There is a considerable amount of controversy regarding the removal of the older rams by hunting. Although there is little evidence at present to suggest it is having a detrimental effect, it must be assumed that, in any species, breeding should be carried out by the strongest.

Thinhorn are generally hunted in late summer and autumn. As a rule, only rams with full-curl horns or larger may be taken, although in some areas slightly smaller animals are allowed. Once a large ram has been spied amongst a herd, the stalk may prove to be extremely hard work with a considerable amount of climbing. However, the white coat of the Dall's sheep allows the herd to be located rather more easily, except in snow. If the hunter is fit, he should be successful.

Some ewe hunting is allowed but many feel that not enough is being done to manage the population in accordance with the available habitat. Herds should be controlled below the level of the carrying capacity of their range by the culling of ewes rather than just the big rams. This should produce greater reproduction, survival and, therefore, growth rates. However, there is some difficulty in convincing both hunters and many biologists who consider mountain sheep as sacred animals to which normal husbandry rules do not apply.

# American Black Bear
## (URSUS AMERICANUS)

THE BLACK BEAR'S RANGE covers most of Canada and Alaska, much of western and parts of eastern United States and northern Mexico. Their historical range has constricted due to hunting pressure and habitat loss but controlled shooting and forest management – mostly incidental – have resulted in an overall stable or increasing population. Where habitat loss continues, the black bear is still declining.

The black bear is smaller than brown and grizzly bears, the largest standing about 3ft at the shoulder. There are various colour phases, from black, through brown and cinnamon, to white, but the brown-muzzled black phase is the most common. Black bears are most easily

identified by the straight back and straighter facial profile. Brown and grizzly bears have longer coats, a distinct shoulder hump and a prominent forehead bump.

Black bears are active mostly during the day though they can be nocturnal. They live within a large home range, covering a diverse variety of forest habitat – deciduous, coniferous or mixed – both in mountainous and lowland regions. Natural forest with mixed aged trees is favoured, the bears using different areas at

different times of the year – perhaps taking advantage of an acorn supply for a week or so before moving on. Although their diet is predominantly vegetarian, black bears are omnivorous, eating a wide variety of berries, forest mast, roots, bark, grasses, carrion, insects, rodents and, occasionally, livestock. They are greatly attracted to rubbish tips and, as such, can often be found close to towns and cities, whilst the brown and grizzly have retreated away from man.

The breeding season is in June and July

during which the boar moves from one sow to another. Outside this period, boars and cubless sows become solitary – a necessary precaution as the boar, given the chance, would eat the cubs. Sows usually start breeding at 4–5 years old – 3 years at the earliest – and generally produce litters in alternate years. The cubs, commonly 2–3 but sometimes 5–6 in ideal habitat, are born in the den in January or February. Independent at 8–10 months, the cubs will not usually leave the sow until she has her next litter. Timber wolves probably offer the biggest threat as predators although black bears are excellent tree climbers and can usually escape.

Black bears retire to their dens for a partial hibernation between November and April. The den is often a burrow, cave or hole amongst tree roots, though sometimes bears dig into the snow or simply lie on the ground and let the snow cover them. Mainly living off fat reserves accumulated in the autumn, black bears can, nevertheless, venture out to forage for food, especially in the south where dens are less commonly used. During the summer, they tend to curl up on the forest floor, in shady areas, to sleep.

Black bears are generally hunted in spring and autumn, both as a trophy and for the meat. Hunters generally take advantage of their feeding habits, either waiting up near a traditionally used area or baiting with meat, fish or sugary foods. They may be stalked within the forest, though most states prohibit the disturbance of their dens so the hunter will need to know their movements well. Still practised by some is the rather more predictable method of hunting with dogs, the gun following in their wake and shooting once the animal has been treed. Attacks on humans do occasionally occur, especially by animals in poor condition, stressed by food shortage.

# Snowshoe Hare (LEPUS AMERICANUS)

THE SNOWSHOE OR VARYING hare is found in the forested parts of Canada, Alaska and northern United States. Generally, their range corresponds with that of the ruffed grouse, though extending further north and not as far south. The snowshoe's cycle is largely responsible for that of the ruffed grouse. At peak numbers, all the available food is consumed and the population subsequently crashes. The slow recovery begins whilst the increased dependent predators concentrate on the ruffed grouse. The ruffed grouse crash, the predators crash and the cycle begins again.

In autumn, the snowshoe hare's brown summer coat gradually changes to pure white – except for the barely perceptible black tips of the ears – and the feet become thickly furred, enabling it to run across soft snow with relative ease. During the spring the coat changes back, offering it year-round camouflage.

Living above ground and inhabiting both mountainous and lowland areas, the snowshoe hare prefers coniferous or mixed forest and brushy bogs, rarely being found in purely deciduous woodland or on farmland, unless there are plenty of woods and bogs nearby. Their diet, consisting of grassy and weedy vegetation in summer, changes to twigs, buds and bark in winter when there is little else available above the snow.

Like the European brown hare, the snowshoes box with each other in the spring. The breeding season commences in about April and continues until September. They are polygamous and the buck, staying with each

Snowshoe hare

doe in turn until mated, plays no part in raising the litter. The doe can produce 5 litters in a good year – and even 3–4 in a poor one – each with 4–6 leverets born above ground, furred and with their eyes open. The doe visits the young in the well-concealed form and they are soon able to fend for themselves, as they must before she produces her next litter. Snowshoe predators include lynx, coyotes, foxes, eagles, hawks and owls. Ignoring the enormous fluctuations of the cycle, the population is thought to be stable in Canada and declining in the United States.

Whilst bag limits generally apply, there are many areas which offer no close season for snowshoe hares. They are little hunted for sport, though large numbers are taken each year for food, especially in Canada.

Whilst they are sometimes shot by bird hunters, those with dogs tend to leave them or else risk encouraging their dogs to chase them. Therefore, on the whole, the hunter specifically sets out after hares and either still-hunts them through the woods or uses beagles to trail them, shooting when the hare finally stops. Both shotguns and rifles are used.

# Cottontail Rabbit
## (SYLVILAGUS FLORIDANUS)

FOUND THROUGHOUT THE UNITED STATES and in parts of southern Canada, the cottontail is the most abundant and widespread of the North American rabbits. However, their numbers fluctuate, mainly because of hunting and predation, and the population is thought to be stable, at best.

Cottontail rabbit

The cottontail is very similar in appearance to the European rabbit, having a brown coat with a white belly and scut, though perhaps on average a little smaller. Cottontail habitat varies enormously, depending on the area, and includes farmland, woodland, brushy areas and semi-desert scrub. Outside the breeding season they are generally solitary and live above ground, only resorting to holes when escaping predators or, occasionally in cold weather when they may also burrow into deep powdery snow for warmth. Their diet consists of a wide variety of grasses, weedy and shrubby vegetation, arable crops and, in winter, the twigs and bark of trees and shrubs.

Breeding between February and September, the bucks fight for and pursue each doe in turn. Does may have up to 6 litters of 4–5 young which are born blind and naked in a fur and grass-lined scrape or shallow hole, hidden in moderate cover. They are confined to the nest for 10 days or so, totally reliant on the doe, and thereafter gradually become more independent. The cottontail's size makes it a very manageable prey for a great many predators, from weasels to hawks, which explains the need for such tenacious breeding habits.

*Hunting seasons fall between October and February.*

Whilst jack rabbits, found in the western states, can be a pest and are often controlled by driven shooting, cottontails are considered 'game' with hunters setting out specifically to shoot them, using shotguns or rifles. In most states, lamping at night is illegal and they are mainly walked up, either with or without dogs. Some states do not set bag limits.

# Index

# _L_atin/English

|  |  |
|-------|---------|
| Alces alces alces | elk, European |
| Alectoris chukar | chukar |
| Alectoris graeca | partridge, rock |
| Alectoris rufa | partridge, red-legged |
| Anas acuta | pintail |
| Anas crecca | teal |
| Anas penelope | wigeon |
| Anas platyrhyncos | mallard |
| Anas strepera | gadwall |
| Anser albifrons flavirostris | goose, Greenland, white-fronted |
| Anser albifrons | goose, white-fronted |
| Anser anser | goose, greylag |
| Anser brachyrhynchus | goose, pink-footed |
| Antilocapra americana | pronghorn |
| Aythya ferina | pochard |
| Aythya fuligula | tufted |
| Aythya marila | scaup |
| Bonasa bonasia | grouse, hazel |
| Bonasa umbellus | grouse, ruffed |
| Branta canadensis | goose, Canada |
| Bucephala clangula | goldeneye |
| Callipepla californicus | quail, California |
| Capra ibex ibex | Alpine ibex |
| Capra pyrenaica | Spanish ibex |
| Capreolus capreolus | deer, roe |
| Centrocercus urophasianus | grouse, sage |
| Cervus elaphus | deer, red |
| Cervus elaphus | deer, wapiti |
| Cervus nippon | deer, sika |
| Colinus virginianus | quail, northern bobwhite |
| Columba livia | pigeon, feral |
| Columba palumbus | woodpigeon |
| Corvus corone cornix | crow, hooded |
| Corvus corone corone | crow, carrion |
| Corvus frugilegus | rook |
| Corvus monedula | jackdaw |
| Coturnix coturnix | quail, European migratory |
| Dama dama | deer, fallow |
| Dendragapus canadensis | grouse, spruce |
| Dendragapus obscurus | grouse, blue |
| Fulica atra | coot |
| Gallinago gallinago | snipe |
| Gallinula chloropus | moorhen |
| Garrulus glandarius | jay |
| Hydropotes inermis | deer, Chinese water |
| Lagopus lagopus hibernicus | grouse, Irish red |
| Lagopus lagopus lagopus | grouse, Scandinavian, willow |
| Lagopus lagopus scoticus | grouse, red |
| Lagopus mutus | ptarmigan |
| Larus argentatus | gull, herring |
| Larus fuscus | gull, lesser, black-backed |
| Larus marinus | gull, great, black-backed |
| Lepus americanus | hare, snowshoe |
| Lepus europaeus | hare, brown |
| Lepus timidus hibernicus | hare, Irish |
| Lepus timidus scoticus | hare, blue |
| Lutreola vison | mink |
| Lymnocryptes minimus | snipe, jack |
| Meleagris gallopavo | turkey, wild |
| Muntiacus reevesi | Reeves muntjac |
| Mustela erminea | stoat |
| Mustela nivalis | weasel |
| Numenius arquata | curlew |
| Odocoileus hermionus | deer, mule |
| Odocoileus virginianus | deer, white-tailed |
| Oryctolagus cuniculus | rabbit |
| Ovis canadensis | sheep, bighorn |
| Ovis dalli dalli | sheep, Dall's, thinhorn |
| Ovis dalli | sheep, thinhorn, |
| Ovis dalli stonei | sheep, Stone's, thinhorn |
| Ovis musimon | sheep, European mouflon |
| Passer domesticus | house sparrow |
| Perdix perdix | partridge, grey |
| Phasianus colchicus | pheasant |
| Pica pica | magpie |
| Pluvialis apricaria | plover, golden |
| Rattus norvegicus | rat |
| Rupicapra rupicapra | chamois |
| Sciurus carolinensis | squirrel, grey |
| Scolopax minor | woodcock, American |
| Scolopax rusticola | woodcock |
| Spatula clypeata | duck, shoveler |
| Streptopelia decaocto | dove, collared |
| Streptopelia turtur | dove, turtle |
| Sturnus vulgaris | starling |
| Sus scrofa | wild boar |
| Sylvilagus floridanus | rabbit, cottontail |
| Tetrao tetrix | grouse, black |
| Tetrao urogallus | capercaillie |
| Tympanuchus cupido pinnatus | prairie chicken, greater |
| Tympanuchus phasianellus | grouse, sharp-tailed |
| Ursus americanus | bear, American black |
| Vulpes vulpes | fox |
| Zenaida macroura | dove, mourning |